Published by
Rupa Publications India Pvt. Ltd 2025
7/16, Ansari Road, Daryaganj
New Delhi 110002

Sales centres:
Bengaluru Chennai
Hyderabad Jaipur Kathmandu
Kolkata Mumbai Prayagraj

Copyright © Rupa Publications India Pvt. Ltd 2025

The views and opinions expressed in this book are the
authors' own and the facts are as reported by him which
have been verified to the extent possible, and the publishers
are not in any way liable for the same.

All rights reserved.
No part of this publication may be reproduced, transmitted,
or stored in a retrieval system, in any form or by any means,
electronic, mechanical, photocopying, recording or otherwise,
without the prior permission of the publisher.

Photo Source: Wikimedia Commons

ISBN: 978-93-6156-147-4

First impression 2025

10 9 8 7 6 5 4 3 2 1

The moral right of the author has been asserted.

Printed in India

This book is sold subject to the condition that it shall not,
by way of trade or otherwise, be lent, resold, hired out, or otherwise
circulated, without the publisher's prior consent, in any form of
binding or cover other than that in which it is published.

CONTENTS

Introduction		5
1	The History of Weight lifting	8

SECTION ONE
GETTING STARTED

2	Understanding Weight lifting	24
3	Equipment and Gear	36
4	Basic Weight-Lifting Techniques	51

SECTION TWO
CORE LIFTS AND TECHNIQUES

5	The Squat	58
6	The Deadlift	65
7	The Bench Press	74
8	The Overhead Press	80

SECTION THREE
ADVANCED TECHNIQUES AND TRAINING

9	Accessory Lifts and Their Role	86
10	Advanced Lifting Techniques	99
11	Programming for Strength and Hypertrophy	105

SECTION FOUR
NUTRITION AND RECOVERY

12	Nutrition for Weight-Lifting	112
13	The Importance of Recovery	119

SECTION FIVE
THE MENTAL GAME AND COMPETITION

14	The Psychology of Weight-Lifting	128
15	Preparing for Competitions	135
16	Analyzing Performance and Continuous Improvement	140
17.	Nurturing a Future Olympic Weightlifter	145
18.	Filipino Olympians in Weightlifting: Lifting the Nation	149
	Conclusion	153
	List of Olympic Medalists (2000–2024)	154

INTRODUCTION

WEIGHT LIFTING IS MORE THAN JUST MOVING heavy objects—it's a discipline that embodies strength, resilience, and a deep commitment to personal growth. Whether you're an aspiring athlete, a fitness enthusiast, or someone looking to improve your health, Weight lifting offers a transformative experience that goes beyond physical gains. This book is designed to be your comprehensive guide, leading you through the essential principles, techniques, and strategies of Weight lifting to help you reach your goals.

In today's fitness landscape, Weight lifting has gained unprecedented popularity. No longer confined to the hardcore environments of bodybuilding gyms, it has become a mainstream pursuit, embraced by people of all ages and backgrounds. This surge in popularity is driven by a growing recognition of the benefits of strength training, not just for athletic performance but also for overall health and well-being. From increasing bone density and improving metabolic function to enhancing mental health and longevity, the advantages of incorporating Weight lifting into your fitness routine are well-documented and widely endorsed by experts across various fields.

One of the most exciting aspects of Weight lifting today is its accessibility. Advances in fitness technology, online resources, and social media have democratized the sport, making expert knowledge and coaching available to everyone. Whether you train at a state-of-the-art facility, a modest home gym, or even a local park, the tools and information you need to succeed are within reach. This book taps into this wealth of resources, providing you with the latest insights and practical advice to ensure you make the most of your Weight lifting journey.

This book is structured to cater to both beginners and seasoned lifters. If you're new to the sport, you'll find step-by-step instructions on mastering the fundamentals, from understanding basic movements to setting realistic goals. For more experienced lifters, advanced techniques and strategies are detailed to help you break through plateaus and continue progressing. Regardless of where you are on your lifting journey, the principles outlined here will guide you in building a solid foundation and achieving long-term success.

One of the key themes of this book is the importance of proper form and technique. In an era where quick fixes and shortcuts are often promoted, we emphasize the value of doing things the right way. Proper technique not only maximizes the effectiveness of your workouts but also significantly reduces the risk of injury, ensuring you can lift for years to come. The book also explores the mental aspects of Weight lifting, acknowledging that physical strength is closely tied to mental fortitude. You'll learn how to cultivate the mindset of a successful lifter, building the resilience and focus needed to overcome challenges both in and out of the gym.

Furthermore, the book addresses the increasingly important topics of nutrition and recovery. As the science of sports nutrition evolves, so does our understanding of how to fuel the body for optimal performance and recovery. The guidance provided here is based on the latest research, helping you navigate the complex world of diets, supplements, and recovery protocols to find what works best for you.

Finally, this book celebrates the community and culture of Weight lifting. In a sport that can sometimes seem solitary, the sense of camaraderie and shared purpose among lifters is invaluable. Whether you lift alone or with others, being part of the Weight lifting community offers support, motivation, and a wealth of shared knowledge. As you progress through this book, you'll not only develop as a lifter but also gain a deeper appreciation for the sport and the people who dedicate themselves to it.

Weight lifting is a lifelong journey, and this book is your companion along the way. Whether your goal is to compete, improve your physique, or simply become stronger, the knowledge and tools provided here will empower you to reach your full potential.

1

THE HISTORY OF WEIGHT LIFTING

Weightlifting pictogram

WEIGHT LIFTING HAS A DEEP AND RICH HISTORY, tracing its roots back thousands of years to when humans first began to challenge one another in feats of strength. What began as primal displays of physical power has evolved into a sophisticated sport and essential component of modern fitness regimes. The journey of Weight lifting reflects humanity's enduring pursuit of physical and mental mastery, as well as the sport's adaptability to cultural shifts and technological advancements. Exploring this history offers insight into how Weight lifting has developed into the diverse and respected practice it is today.

Origins of Weight lifting

The origins of Weight lifting can be traced back to ancient civilizations, where lifting heavy objects was a common way to demonstrate strength and endurance. In ancient Egypt, depictions of soldiers lifting heavy stones are found in hieroglyphics, suggesting that Weight lifting was part of military training, possibly to prepare warriors for the rigors of combat. Similarly, in ancient Greece, the lifting of large stones was a popular method of testing and showcasing physical strength, often performed in preparation for athletic competitions. These early practices, although not formalized, laid the groundwork for the sport's development.

Greek mythology also played a role in shaping early perceptions of strength. Figures like Heracles, known for his superhuman strength, became cultural icons, embodying the ideal of physical power and prowess. Such mythological narratives helped to elevate the importance of physical strength in society, influencing the early development of strength-based competitions. The ancient Greeks also introduced the concept of physical fitness as a component of education, with young men trained in gyms (or "gymnasia") where lifting and other strength-building exercises were a regular part of their regimen.

Heracles

In ancient China, Weight lifting was practiced as part of military training, where soldiers were expected to lift heavy weights to prepare for battle. This practice was not merely a test of strength but also a method to ensure that soldiers were physically prepared for the demands of warfare. The use of Weight lifting as a tool for building strength was widespread, with records of soldiers lifting weights as early as the Zhou Dynasty (1046–256 BCE). The Chinese also used various forms of resistance training, including lifting stone locks, which resemble modern-day kettlebells.

These early forms of Weight lifting, though rudimentary, highlight a common thread across different cultures: the recognition of strength as a vital attribute, not just for survival but for social status and personal pride. The competitive aspect of lifting heavy objects would eventually evolve into more formalized sports, but these early practices laid the foundation for what would become modern Weight lifting.

Evolution of the Sport and Its Different Forms

As societies progressed, the practice of Weight lifting became more organized and formalized, eventually evolving into the structured disciplines we recognize today. The 19th century marked a significant turning point in the evolution of Weight lifting, particularly with the rise of strongman competitions in Europe. These competitions often featured performers who showcased their strength by lifting and carrying heavy objects, bending iron bars, and performing other extraordinary feats. Strongmen like Eugen Sandow, often hailed as the father of modern bodybuilding, played a pivotal role in popularizing Weight lifting as both a form of entertainment and a serious athletic pursuit.

Eugen Sandow, a German-born strongman, was instrumental in transforming Weight lifting from a mere spectacle into a disciplined practice. Sandow's performances, which included lifting heavy dumbbells and barbells, drew large crowds across Europe and the United States. He emphasized the importance of physical conditioning and muscular development, which was a departure from the traditional strongman focus on sheer brute strength. Sandow's influence extended beyond his time on stage; he published books on physical culture, founded one of the first commercial gyms, and even inspired the creation of the International Federation of Bodybuilding & Fitness (IFBB). His legacy is still celebrated today, with the "Mr. Olympia" trophy named in his honor.

OLYMPIC SERIES: WEIGHT LIFTING

Image: Eugen Sandow

The late 19th and early 20th centuries saw the formalization of Weight lifting as a competitive sport. The first official World Weightlifting Championships were held in 1891 in London, setting the stage for the sport's global recognition. At the inaugural event, seven athletes competed in various lifting categories, showcasing their strength through different lifts, including the one-handed lift and the two-handed lift. This competition laid the groundwork for future international events and established the rules and standards for competitive Weight lifting.

Weight lifting made its Olympic debut at the first modern Olympic Games in Athens in 1896, featuring both one-handed and two-handed lifts. Although it was not included in the 1900 Paris Games, it returned in 1904 and has been a permanent fixture in the Olympics since 1920. Over time, the sport evolved to focus on two main lifts: the snatch and the clean & jerk, both of which require not only strength but also speed, technique, and precision. These lifts became the standard events in Olympic Weight lifting, and the sport has continued to grow in popularity and prestige.

THE HISTORY OF WEIGHT LIFTING

1896 Athens Summer Olympics

Weigthlifter Oscar Osthoff at the 1904 Summer Olympics

OLYMPIC SERIES: WEIGHT LIFTING

Fred Winters at the 1904 Olympics, lifting weight

The Snatch Lift

THE HISTORY OF WEIGHT LIFTING

The Clean & Jerk Lift

Parallel to Olympic Weight lifting, other forms of the sport began to emerge. **Powerlifting**, which emphasizes maximal strength through the squat, bench press, and deadlift, developed in the mid-20th century. Unlike Olympic Weight lifting, which involves dynamic lifts performed in a single explosive movement, powerlifting focuses on moving the heaviest possible weight in a controlled manner. The first national powerlifting championships were held in the United States in 1965, and the sport quickly gained a dedicated following. Today, powerlifting is practiced worldwide, with its own set of rules, competitions, and governing bodies.

Powerlifting at Invictus Games

Bodybuilder

Bodybuilding emerged as a distinct form of Weight lifting, focusing not only on strength but also on muscle size, symmetry, and definition. Pioneers like Sandow laid the groundwork, but it wasn't until the mid-20th century that bodybuilding truly took off. The establishment of the IFBB in 1946 by brothers Joe and Ben Weider helped to standardize the sport and promote it internationally. The introduction of the Mr. Olympia competition in 1965 provided a platform for bodybuilders to showcase their physiques and propelled the sport into the mainstream. Figures like Arnold Schwarzenegger, who won seven Mr. Olympia titles, became global icons and helped to popularize Weight lifting as a vital component of fitness culture.

These distinct forms of Weight lifting—Olympic Weight lifting, powerlifting, and bodybuilding—each have their own unique cultures, techniques, and competitive formats. Together, they have contributed to the widespread appeal and accessibility of Weight lifting as a sport and fitness practice, catering to a diverse range of goals and interests.

NOTABLE LIFTERS AND HISTORICAL MILESTONES

Throughout the history of Weight lifting, certain individuals have stood out as pioneers, legends, and record-breakers. Their contributions have not only advanced the sport but also inspired countless others to take up the challenge of lifting. These notable lifters and their achievements are celebrated for their impact on both the sport and the broader fitness community.

Eugen Sandow, Portrait

Eugen Sandow is often regarded as the first modern bodybuilder and a pioneer of physical culture. His approach to Weight lifting and bodybuilding emphasized the importance of symmetry, proportion, and muscle definition, which set him apart from the traditional strongmen of his time who focused solely on brute strength. Sandow's influence extended far beyond his performances; he authored several books on physical fitness, established a successful mail-order business selling fitness equipment, and opened gyms that promoted his methods of training. His legacy is commemorated in the Mr. Olympia competition, where the winner receives the Sandow trophy.

Paul Anderson, known as one of the strongest men in history, was an American weight-lifter and powerlifter who dominated the sport in the 1950s. Anderson won the gold medal in Weight lifting at the 1956 Melbourne Olympics and set numerous world records in both Olympic Weight lifting and powerlifting. His feats of strength were legendary, including an unofficial backlift of 6,270 pounds, a record that remains unmatched. Anderson's contributions to strength sports went beyond his competitive career; he also founded the Paul Anderson Youth Home, a charitable organization that helps troubled youth through strength training and discipline.

Paul Anderson

Vasily Alekseyev, a Soviet weight-lifter, became a dominant force in the sport during the 1970s. Competing in the super-heavyweight division, Alekseyev set 80 world records and won gold medals at the 1972 Munich and 1976 Montreal Olympics. His unparalleled success brought significant attention to Olympic Weight lifting and inspired a generation of lifters in the Soviet Union and beyond. Alekseyev's training methods and psychological approach to competition were groundbreaking, and his influence can still be seen in the sport today.

Vasily Alekseyev

In the world of bodybuilding, **Arnold Schwarzenegger** stands as a monumental figure. His rise to fame in the 1970s, with seven Mr. Olympia titles and a successful transition to Hollywood, helped bring bodybuilding into the mainstream. Schwarzenegger's impact on the sport is profound; he not only set new standards for muscle development and symmetry but also helped to popularize Weight lifting as a key component of general fitness. His autobiography, "Arnold: The Education of a Bodybuilder," and his role in the documentary "Pumping Iron" inspired

Arnold Schwarzenegger

millions to take up Weight lifting, and his influence on the fitness industry continues to this day.

THE ROLE OF WEIGHT LIFTING IN MODERN FITNESS

In the 21st century, Weight lifting has become a cornerstone of modern fitness. Its benefits extend far beyond the realm of competitive sports, making it an essential practice for people of all ages and fitness levels. The growing body of research on strength training has highlighted its numerous health benefits, which include improving bone density, enhancing metabolic function, reducing the risk of chronic diseases, and promoting mental well-being.

As the understanding of fitness has evolved, Weight lifting has shed its image as an activity only for bodybuilders or athletes. Today, strength training is widely recommended by health professionals as a key component of a balanced exercise program. Its applications are broad, from functional training that improves everyday movement patterns to specialized programs designed for rehabilitation and injury prevention. Weight lifting has also been shown to have significant psychological benefits, including reducing symptoms of depression and anxiety, improving self-esteem, and fostering a sense of empowerment.

The accessibility of Weight lifting has also increased dramatically. The rise of digital fitness platforms, online coaching, and social media has made expert knowledge and training resources available to anyone with an internet connection. These platforms have democratized Weight lifting, allowing individuals from all walks of life to learn proper techniques, track their progress, and connect with a global community of lifters. The social aspect of Weight lifting, whether through online forums or local gyms, provides a sense of camaraderie and support that enhances the overall experience.

In addition to traditional Weight lifting practices, the fitness industry has seen the rise of **functional training**, which incorporates Weight lifting movements into routines designed to mimic real-life activities. This approach has made strength training more relevant and accessible to the general population, emphasizing the importance of building strength for everyday tasks and overall health. Movements like squats, deadlifts, and presses are now commonly included in workout programs aimed at improving posture, balance, and mobility, making Weight lifting an integral part of functional fitness.

The impact of technology on Weight lifting cannot be overstated. Innovations such as wearable fitness trackers, smart gym equipment, and strength-training apps have made it easier than ever to monitor progress, optimize workouts, and reduce the risk of injury. These tools provide real-time feedback and data-driven insights that help lifters improve their performance and achieve their goals more efficiently. Virtual coaching and online competitions have also emerged, allowing lifters to participate in the sport regardless of their geographic location, further expanding the reach and inclusivity of Weight lifting.

Weight lifting has also become a vital tool in the fight against aging. Research has shown that strength training is one of the most effective ways to combat the natural decline in muscle mass, bone density, and metabolic rate that occurs with age. As a result, Weight lifting is increasingly recommended for older adults as a means of maintaining independence, preventing falls, and improving overall quality of life. This shift has led to a growing number of older adults embracing Weight lifting, with many experiencing significant improvements in their physical and mental health.

The role of Weight lifting in modern fitness continues to evolve, with new trends and practices emerging regularly. Whether it's the integration of Weight lifting into high-intensity interval training (HIIT), the growing popularity of powerlifting and Olympic Weight lifting as recreational activities, or the increasing focus on sustainable and injury-preventive training methods, Weight lifting remains at the forefront of the fitness world. Its versatility and proven benefits ensure that it will continue to be a cornerstone of fitness for generations to come, helping individuals of all ages and abilities to achieve their physical and mental potential.

SECTION ONE
GETTING STARTED

2

UNDERSTANDING WEIGHT LIFTING

WEIGHT LIFTING IS A VERSATILE AND POWERFUL tool for transforming the body, building strength, and improving overall fitness. It's more than just lifting heavy objects—it's a science and an art form, with various techniques and styles designed to achieve specific goals. This chapter delves into the core concepts of Weight lifting, exploring what it is, the different types, essential rules and safety guidelines, and how to set effective goals tailored to individual needs.

WHAT IS WEIGHT LIFTING?

At its core, Weight lifting involves exerting force against resistance, typically in the form of weights, to build muscle strength, endurance, and size. It is one of the oldest forms of exercise, dating back thousands of years, and has evolved into a structured and highly effective practice used by athletes, bodybuilders, and fitness enthusiasts worldwide. Weight lifting isn't just about increasing muscle mass; it also enhances metabolic health, bone density, and overall physical capability.

The essence of Weight lifting lies in progressive overload, a principle where the muscles are gradually subjected to greater resistance, forcing them to adapt by growing stronger and larger. This can be achieved through various exercises that target different muscle groups, using equipment such as dumbbells, barbells, kettlebells, and machines. Weight lifting is highly adaptable, allowing individuals to tailor their workouts to meet specific fitness goals, whether it's to increase strength, build muscle, or improve overall fitness.

The beauty of Weight lifting lies in its versatility. It can be integrated into any fitness routine, whether you are a beginner looking to improve general fitness or an advanced lifter aiming to compete in powerlifting or bodybuilding. Understanding the different types of Weight lifting and their applications is crucial for maximizing the benefits of this powerful form of exercise.

TYPES OF WEIGHT LIFTING

Weight lifting encompasses several distinct disciplines, each with its own unique focus and techniques. The most common types include powerlifting, Olympic Weight lifting, bodybuilding, and functional training. Each discipline offers different benefits and appeals to different types of lifters, depending on their goals.

Powerlifting

Powerlifting is a strength sport that revolves around three main lifts: the squat, bench press, and deadlift. The goal is to lift as much weight as possible in each of these movements. Powerlifting is all about raw strength, and it's a discipline that requires not only physical power but also mental focus and resilience. Training typically involves lifting heavy weights for low repetitions, with a strong emphasis on technique and form to maximize the amount of weight lifted safely.

Powerlifting

Olympic Weight Lifting

Olympic Weight lifting, often simply referred to as Weight lifting, is an Olympic sport that focuses on two explosive movements: the snatch and the clean & jerk. Unlike powerlifting, which emphasizes maximal strength, Olympic Weight lifting requires a combination of strength, speed, and technique. The snatch involves lifting the barbell from the ground to overhead in one smooth motion, while the clean & jerk is a two-part lift where the barbell is first brought to the shoulders (clean) and then pushed overhead (jerk).

Olympic lifting is highly technical and requires precise coordination, making it one of the most challenging yet rewarding forms of Weight lifting.

Olympic Weight Lifting

Bodybuilding

Bodybuilding is the pursuit of muscular hypertrophy, or muscle growth, with the aim of achieving a well-defined, symmetrical physique. Unlike powerlifting and Olympic lifting, bodybuilding is not just about how much weight you can lift but how effectively you can stimulate muscle growth. This involves a combination of heavy lifting and high-repetition exercises to target and develop specific muscle groups. Bodybuilders often follow strict training and nutrition regimens to reduce body fat and enhance muscle definition, culminating in competitions where they are judged on their physique.

Body Building

Functional Training

Functional training incorporates Weight lifting movements into exercises that mimic real-life activities, focusing on improving overall strength, balance, and coordination. This type of training is often used to enhance athletic performance and daily functional abilities, making it a popular choice for those looking to improve their general fitness and quality of life. Exercises in functional training often involve multiple muscle groups and joints, promoting a more integrated approach to strength training.

Functional training

CrossFit

CrossFit is a high-intensity fitness program that combines elements of Weight lifting, cardio, and bodyweight exercises into varied, functional movements performed at high intensity. CrossFit workouts often include Olympic lifts, powerlifting movements, and other strength-based exercises as part of a broader fitness regimen. The focus is on overall fitness, with an emphasis on functional strength, endurance, and agility. CrossFit has popularized Weight lifting as part of a comprehensive fitness routine, attracting a diverse range of participants.

CrossFit

THE BASIC RULES AND SAFETY GUIDELINES

Weight lifting is highly effective but can also be dangerous if not done correctly. Adhering to basic rules and safety guidelines is essential to prevent injuries and ensure long-term success in lifting. These principles apply to all forms of Weight lifting, regardless of the specific goals or types of training.

1. **Proper Form and Technique:** The cornerstone of safe and effective Weight lifting is proper form and technique. Each lift has a specific form that must be followed to engage the correct muscles and avoid unnecessary strain on joints and ligaments. For example, when performing a squat, it's crucial to maintain a neutral spine, keep the knees aligned with the toes, and lower the hips below the knees while keeping the chest up. Mastering the correct form is especially important when lifting heavy weights, as improper technique can lead to serious injuries.

Form and Technique

2. **Warm-Up and Cool-Down:** Before starting any Weight lifting session, a proper warm-up is essential. This should include light aerobic activity to increase blood flow and dynamic stretches to prepare the muscles and joints for the workout. A cool-down after the workout, including stretching and light activity, helps to gradually bring the heart rate down and aids in recovery, reducing muscle stiffness and soreness.

Warm-Up before a session

3. **Progressive Overload:** To make consistent gains in strength and muscle size, the principle of progressive overload must be applied. This involves gradually increasing the weight, repetitions, or intensity of your workouts to continually challenge your muscles. However, progression should be incremental to avoid overloading the muscles and joints too quickly, which can lead to injury.

Progressive Overload

4. **Rest and Recovery:** Adequate rest and recovery are just as important as the lifting itself. Muscles grow and repair during rest, so it's essential to allow enough time between workouts for recovery. Overtraining can lead to fatigue, decreased performance, and increased risk of injury. A well-rounded Weight lifting program should include rest days and active recovery sessions, such as light cardio or stretching, to promote muscle repair and prevent burnout.

5. **Nutrition and Hydration:** Proper nutrition fuels your workouts and supports recovery. A balanced diet that includes sufficient protein, carbohydrates, and fats is essential for muscle repair and growth. Hydration is also crucial, as lifting weights depletes your body's fluids through sweat. Drinking enough water before, during, and after workouts helps maintain performance and supports recovery.
6. **Listening to Your Body:** Weight lifting should be challenging, but it's important to listen to your body and recognize the difference between pushing through discomfort and risking injury. If you experience sharp pain, dizziness, or extreme fatigue, it's a sign to stop and assess the situation. Pushing through serious pain can lead to long-term injuries that could sideline your progress.

SETTING GOALS: STRENGTH, HYPERTROPHY, ENDURANCE

Setting clear and realistic goals is crucial for a successful Weight lifting journey. Whether your objective is to increase strength, build muscle, or improve endurance, having specific targets helps guide your training and keeps you motivated.

1. **Strength:** For those focused on building strength, the goal is to lift heavier weights over time. Strength training typically involves low repetitions with heavy weights, focusing on compound movements like squats, deadlifts, and bench presses. Setting goals in strength training might include lifting a certain amount of weight

or mastering a specific lift. Tracking your progress through a training log can help keep you on track and highlight areas for improvement.

2. **Hypertrophy:** If muscle growth, or hypertrophy, is your goal, the focus shifts to volume and intensity. Hypertrophy training usually involves moderate to heavy weights with higher repetitions, targeting specific muscle groups with a variety of exercises. Goals in hypertrophy might include increasing the size of specific muscles, improving symmetry, or achieving a certain body composition. Progress can be measured through changes in body measurements, muscle definition, and strength levels.

3. **Endurance:** For those looking to improve muscular endurance, the goal is to perform a high number of repetitions with lighter weights. Endurance training is about sustaining effort over time, which can be particularly beneficial for athletes and those looking to improve their overall fitness. Goals might include completing a certain number of repetitions or increasing the duration of a workout without fatigue. Endurance training often incorporates circuit training or high-intensity interval training (HIIT) to challenge both muscular and cardiovascular endurance.

4. **Combination Goals:** Many lifters choose to pursue a combination of these goals, such as building strength while also increasing muscle size or improving endurance. A well-rounded Weight lifting program can incorporate elements of strength, hypertrophy, and endurance training, with specific periods dedicated to each focus. Periodization, or cycling through different

phases of training, can help balance these goals and prevent plateaus.

Understanding the fundamentals of Weight lifting, the different types of lifting, the essential safety guidelines, and how to set and achieve goals lays the groundwork for a successful and rewarding fitness journey. Whether you are new to Weight lifting or an experienced lifter, these principles will help you maximize your results, stay safe, and enjoy the many benefits that Weight lifting has to offer.

3

EQUIPMENT AND GEAR

IN THE WORLD OF WEIGHT-LIFTING, THE RIGHT equipment and gear are crucial not only for achieving your fitness goals but also for ensuring safety and efficiency during workouts. Whether you're lifting in a gym or setting up a home workout space, understanding the essential equipment, how to choose the right gear, and the importance of proper maintenance can make all the difference in your lifting experience. This chapter explores the key pieces of weight-lifting equipment, how to select gear that aligns with your goals, and the role of accessories in enhancing performance and safety.

ESSENTIAL WEIGHT-LIFTING EQUIPMENT: BARBELLS, DUMBBELLS, PLATES, ETC.

The foundation of any weight-lifting regimen lies in the core pieces of equipment: barbells, dumbbells, and weight plates. These tools are indispensable for performing a wide range of exercises that target different muscle groups and allow for progressive overload.

Barbells: Barbells are long metal bars to which weight plates can be attached at either end. They are the cornerstone of weight-lifting and are used in many compound exercises, such as squats, deadlifts, and bench presses. Barbells come in different types, including the standard barbell, Olympic barbell, and specialty bars like the hex bar and EZ curl bar. Olympic barbells are typically longer and heavier than standard barbells and are designed to handle heavier loads. Specialty bars are designed for specific exercises or to accommodate unique grips that can reduce strain on joints.

Barbell

Dumbbells: Dumbbells are short bars with fixed or adjustable weights at each end. They offer greater versatility than barbells, allowing for a broader range of motion and more varied exercises. Dumbbells are particularly useful for unilateral training, where each side of the body is worked independently, helping to correct muscle imbalances. They are also ideal for isolation exercises, such as bicep curls and tricep extensions, and can be used in combination with bodyweight movements for added resistance.

Dumbbells

Weight Plates: Weight plates are discs that are added to barbells and certain types of dumbbells to increase the load. Plates come in various sizes and materials, including cast iron, rubber-coated, and bumper plates. Bumper plates are designed for Olympic lifting, as they can be dropped from height without damaging the floor or the plates themselves. When selecting weight plates, it's important to choose those that are compatible with your barbell and that allow for incremental increases in weight, enabling progressive overload.

Kettlebells: Kettlebells are cast iron or steel balls with handles and are used for a variety of dynamic exercises, such as swings, cleans, and snatches. Unlike dumbbells and barbells, the weight of a kettlebell is offset from its

EQUIPMENT AND GEAR

handle, creating a unique challenge that engages stabilizer muscles and improves functional strength. Kettlebell training is excellent for developing power, endurance, and coordination, making it a valuable addition to any weight-lifting program.

Lifter performing exercise using a 10 kg weight plate

Benches and Racks: A sturdy bench is essential for performing exercises like the bench press, dumbbell rows, and seated shoulder presses. Adjustable benches allow you to change the angle of the backrest, enabling a variety of incline, decline, and flat exercises. Power racks and squat

Kettlebell

racks provide safety and support for heavy lifts, such as squats and overhead presses, by allowing you to set safety bars at an appropriate height to catch the barbell if you fail a lift. They also often feature pull-up bars and other attachments for added versatility.

Bench press

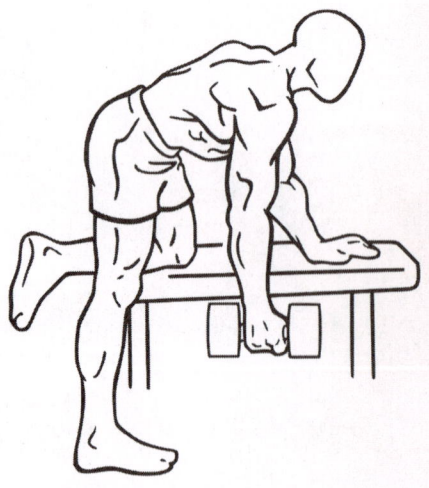

Dumbbell Row;

Seated Shoulder Press

Resistance Bands and Cables: Resistance bands and cable machines provide constant tension throughout the range of motion, making them excellent tools for both assistance and resistance in various exercises. They are particularly useful for warming up, rehabbing injuries, and adding resistance to bodyweight exercises. Bands and cables can also be used in conjunction with free weights to create unique challenges and variations on traditional lifts.

Cable Row Machine

CHOOSING THE RIGHT GEAR FOR YOUR GOALS

Selecting the right gear is essential for aligning your equipment with your specific fitness goals. Whether you're aiming for strength, hypertrophy, endurance, or functional fitness, the gear you choose should support and enhance your training objectives.

For Strength Training: If your primary goal is to build strength, focus on acquiring sturdy, high-quality barbells and weight plates. An Olympic barbell and bumper plates are ideal for heavy lifting, as they can withstand significant loads and the wear and tear of regular use. A power rack with adjustable safety bars is also a must for safe heavy lifting. Investing in a high-quality bench and sturdy dumbbells will round out your strength training setup, allowing you to perform a wide range of exercises with proper support.

EQUIPMENT AND GEAR

A squat safety bar

For Hypertrophy: Those focused on muscle hypertrophy, or muscle growth, should consider a versatile set of dumbbells and a variety of weight plates to allow for incremental increases in resistance. Adjustable dumbbells are a space-saving option that provides a wide range of weights in a single set. A bench with adjustable angles will enable you to target different muscle groups effectively. Incorporating resistance bands and cable attachments can add variety to your workouts, helping you achieve greater muscle activation and growth.

Dumbells and free weights

For Endurance and Functional Fitness: If endurance and functional fitness are your goals, consider incorporating kettlebells, resistance bands, and medicine balls into your routine. These tools are excellent for high-repetition, dynamic movements that build muscular endurance and improve overall functional strength. A lighter set of dumbbells and a pull-up bar can also be beneficial for endurance training, allowing you to perform a variety of bodyweight and resistance exercises.

Medicine Balls

For Home Gyms: When setting up a home gym, space and budget are important considerations. Focus on acquiring versatile, multi-functional equipment that can be used for a variety of exercises. Adjustable dumbbells, resistance bands, a compact bench, and a power rack with pull-up bars can provide a comprehensive setup without taking up too much space. For those with more space and budget, adding a barbell and weight plates, a squat rack, and a cable machine can create a more complete home gym environment.

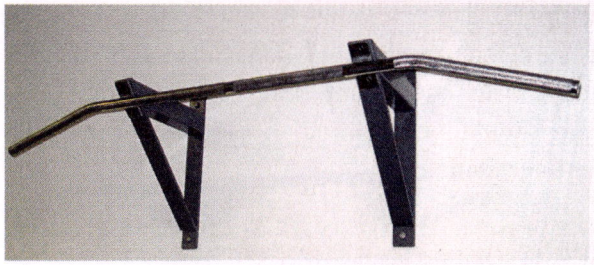

Pull-up bar

MAINTAINING AND CARING FOR YOUR EQUIPMENT

Proper maintenance and care of your weight-lifting equipment are essential for ensuring its longevity and safe use. Regular maintenance not only extends the life of your gear but also ensures that it performs at its best, reducing the risk of accidents and injuries.

Cleaning: Keeping your equipment clean is the first step in maintenance. Wipe down barbells, dumbbells, and kettlebells with a damp cloth after each use to remove sweat, dust, and chalk. For metal equipment, consider using a light coat of oil or lubricant to prevent rust, especially if your gym is in a humid environment. Benches and other padded surfaces should be cleaned with a mild disinfectant to prevent the buildup of bacteria and odors.

Inspecting: Regularly inspect your equipment for signs of wear and tear. Check barbells for any bends or cracks, especially around the collars where plates are loaded. Ensure that weight plates are not chipped or damaged, as this can affect their balance and safety. For adjustable dumbbells, make sure that the locking mechanisms are functioning properly. Any equipment showing significant wear or damage should be repaired or replaced immediately to prevent accidents.

Storing: Proper storage of your equipment is crucial to maintaining its condition. Store barbells on a rack or in a vertical holder to prevent them from warping. Weight plates should be stored on a weight tree or rack, not left on the floor, to prevent damage and reduce the risk of tripping. Dumbbells and kettlebells should be placed on a rack or in a designated area to keep them organized and out of the way. Resistance bands and cables should be hung up or coiled neatly to avoid tangling and unnecessary wear.

Maintaining Accessories: Weight-lifting accessories like belts, straps, and shoes also require care. Belts should be wiped down and stored flat to prevent cracking and warping. Straps should be inspected for fraying and replaced when necessary. Weight-lifting shoes should be kept clean and dry, and their soles should be checked regularly for wear to ensure they provide adequate support and stability during lifts.

THE ROLE OF ACCESSORIES: BELTS, STRAPS, SHOES, ETC.

Weight-lifting accessories play a vital role in enhancing performance, ensuring safety, and providing support during heavy lifts. While not always necessary for every lifter, these accessories can be incredibly beneficial, especially as you advance in your lifting journey.

Belts: Weight-lifting belts are designed to provide support to the lower back and abdominal muscles during heavy lifts, such as squats and deadlifts. By increasing intra-abdominal pressure, belts help stabilize the spine, allowing for safer and more effective lifting. Belts are especially useful when lifting near maximal loads, but they should be used correctly—tightening the belt too much can restrict movement and breathing, while using it too loosely provides little benefit.

Weightlifting belts

Straps: Lifting straps are used to improve grip strength, allowing lifters to hold onto the bar for longer periods, particularly during heavy pulling exercises like deadlifts and rows. Straps wrap around the bar and the lifter's wrist, reducing the load on the hands and forearms. While straps can be incredibly useful, it's important not to rely on them excessively, as developing natural grip strength is also essential for overall lifting performance.

Lifting straps

Shoes: Proper footwear is crucial in weight-lifting. Weight-lifting shoes are designed with a flat, stable sole and a raised heel, which helps improve balance and allows for a more upright posture during squats and other lifts. The solid construction of these shoes provides a stable base, reducing the risk of injury and improving performance. For Olympic lifting, specialized shoes with a higher heel are often used to enhance ankle mobility and provide better positioning for deep squats. Conversely, for deadlifting, some lifters prefer minimalist shoes or even lifting barefoot to maximize ground contact and minimize the distance the bar has to travel.

Weightlifting shoes

Gloves and Grips: Some lifters use gloves or grips to protect their hands and improve grip during lifts. Gloves can prevent calluses and blisters, while grips, often made of leather or synthetic material, provide extra traction on the bar. While these accessories can be helpful, it's important to ensure that they do not interfere with the natural feel of the bar or diminish grip strength.

Weightlifting Gloves

Knee and Elbow Sleeves: Knee and elbow sleeves provide support and compression to the joints, helping to keep them warm and reducing the risk of injury. These sleeves are especially beneficial for lifters who have previous joint injuries or who perform a high volume of squats and presses. The compression from the sleeves can also enhance proprioception, giving lifters a better sense of joint positioning during lifts.

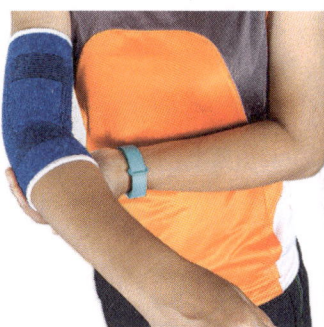

Elbow Sleeves

Chalk: Chalk is used to absorb moisture and improve grip, particularly during heavy lifts like deadlifts and snatches. Applying chalk to the hands reduces slippage and allows for a more secure hold on the bar. While chalk is widely used in powerlifting and Olympic lifting, some gyms may restrict its use due to the mess it can create, so it's essential

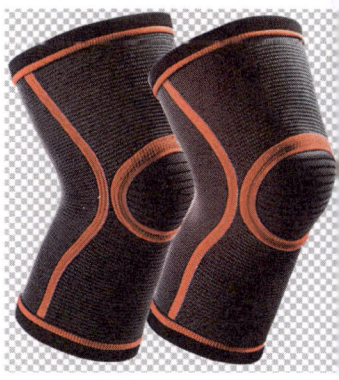

Knee Sleeves

to check gym policies beforehand.

Equipping yourself with the right gear and understanding how to use and maintain it is essential for a safe and successful weight-lifting experience. Whether you're lifting for strength, hypertrophy, or functional fitness, having the proper equipment and accessories can enhance your performance, reduce the risk of injury, and help you achieve your fitness goals more effectively.

4

BASIC WEIGHT-LIFTING TECHNIQUES

MASTERING THE FUNDAMENTAL TECHNIQUES OF weight-lifting is essential for both safety and effectiveness. Whether you're new to lifting or have some experience, understanding proper form, the importance of warm-up and stretching, effective breathing, and common mistakes can dramatically improve your performance and minimize the risk of injury. This chapter provides a comprehensive guide to these core aspects, helping you build a solid foundation for your weight-lifting journey.

UNDERSTANDING PROPER FORM AND TECHNIQUE

Proper form is the cornerstone of safe and effective weight-lifting. Every exercise in your routine should be performed with attention to detail, ensuring that the right muscles are engaged, and the joints are protected. Poor form can lead to inefficient workouts and increase the risk of injury, especially as you begin to lift heavier weights.

KEY PRINCIPLES OF PROPER FORM:

- **Neutral Spine:** Maintaining a neutral spine—where the natural curves of the spine are preserved—is critical in almost all weight-lifting exercises. This position helps distribute the load evenly across the vertebrae and reduces the risk of injury. For exercises like deadlifts and squats, keeping the back straight and avoiding excessive rounding or arching is paramount.
- **Joint Alignment:** Proper joint alignment ensures that your body moves in a safe and efficient way. For example, during a squat, your knees should track over your toes without caving inwards or bowing outwards. Similarly, during pressing movements, such as the bench press or overhead press, your wrists should be stacked directly over your elbows, creating a straight line from the barbell to your shoulder.
- **Controlled Movements:** Weight-lifting isn't about moving the weight from point A to point B as quickly as possible. Instead, focus on controlled movements, which involve both a smooth lift and a controlled lowering phase. This approach not only engages the target muscles more effectively but also reduces the risk of injury.
- **Engaging the Core:** Your core acts as a stabilizer in almost every weight-lifting exercise. Engaging the core—by bracing your abdominal muscles—provides stability and protects the spine during lifts. Whether you're performing a squat, deadlift, or overhead press, a strong core helps maintain proper posture and form.

THE IMPORTANCE OF WARM-UP AND STRETCHING

A proper warm-up is essential before engaging in any weight-lifting session. Warming up prepares the muscles, joints, and nervous system for the demands of lifting, reducing the risk of injury and improving performance.

Dynamic Warm-Up: A dynamic warm-up involves performing exercises that mimic the movements you'll be doing during your workout but at a lower intensity. This might include bodyweight squats, lunges, or arm circles. The goal is to increase blood flow to the muscles, elevate heart rate, and enhance mobility.

Specific Warm-Up Sets: Before lifting heavy, it's advisable to perform a few warm-up sets of the specific exercise you're about to do. Start with lighter weights and gradually increase the load until you reach your working set. For example, if you're planning to squat with 100 kg, you might start with a few sets of 40 kg, then 60 kg, before moving to your target weight.

Stretching: While dynamic stretching is beneficial before lifting, static stretching—where you hold a stretch for a period—can be more effective after your workout. Stretching post-workout helps to lengthen the muscles, improve flexibility, and reduce muscle soreness. Focus on the muscle groups you worked during your session, holding each stretch for 20-30 seconds.

BREATHING TECHNIQUES AND BRACING

Breathing and bracing are often overlooked aspects of weight-lifting, yet they play a critical role in maintaining stability and preventing injury, especially during heavy lifts.

Breathing: The general rule of thumb is to inhale during the eccentric phase (lowering) of the lift and exhale during the concentric phase (lifting). For example, when performing a bench press, inhale as you lower the bar to your chest and exhale as you push it back up. This method ensures that you have enough oxygen to fuel your muscles during the lift while maintaining control of the movement.

Bracing: Bracing involves tightening the core muscles to create intra-abdominal pressure, which stabilizes the spine. To brace effectively, take a deep breath into your belly—not your chest—before starting the lift. Then, tighten your core as if you're preparing to take a punch. This bracing technique is especially important during compound lifts like squats and deadlifts, where spinal stability is crucial.

The Valsalva Maneuver: For very heavy lifts, some lifters use the Valsalva maneuver—a technique where you take a deep breath, hold it, and brace your core while lifting. This maneuver increases intra-abdominal pressure, providing additional support for the spine. However, it should be used cautiously, as holding your breath can cause a temporary spike in blood pressure. It's best to reserve this technique for maximal or near-maximal lifts, and only after you've mastered basic breathing and bracing.

COMMON MISTAKES AND HOW TO AVOID THEM

Even experienced lifters can fall into bad habits over time, leading to suboptimal performance or injury. Being aware of common mistakes and how to correct them is crucial for continuous progress.

Overarching the Lower Back: A common mistake, especially during overhead presses and deadlifts, is overarching the lower back. This places excessive stress on the lumbar spine and can lead to pain or injury. To avoid this, focus on maintaining a neutral spine, engage your core, and squeeze your glutes during the lift to stabilize the pelvis.

Lifting with the Arms Instead of the Legs: In exercises like deadlifts and squats, some lifters mistakenly use their arms to initiate the movement rather than their legs. This reduces the effectiveness of the lift and increases the risk of injury. To correct this, ensure that your legs and hips are driving the movement, with your arms simply holding the bar in place.

Improper Knee Alignment: During squats and lunges, it's common for the knees to cave inwards, especially under heavy load. This can strain the knee joints and lead to injury. To prevent this, focus on pushing your knees outwards as you lower into the squat or lunge, ensuring they track over your toes.

Neglecting the Eccentric Phase: The eccentric phase—when you lower the weight back down—is just as important as the lifting phase. Many lifters rush through this part of the movement, missing out on muscle-building potential and increasing the risk of injury. Instead, focus on controlling the weight during the eccentric phase, taking 2-3 seconds to lower it back down.

Using Too Much Weight Too Soon: One of the biggest mistakes is lifting too much weight before mastering the proper form. This can lead to poor technique and increase the likelihood of injury. Start with a manageable weight that allows you to perform each rep with perfect form, and gradually increase the load as you become more confident and stronger.

Understanding these basic weight-lifting techniques and avoiding common mistakes is key to building a strong, injury-free foundation in your training. Whether your goal is to build strength, improve muscle mass, or enhance overall fitness, focusing on proper form, warming up effectively, and employing correct breathing and bracing techniques will set you up for long-term success.

SECTION TWO

CORE LIFTS AND TECHNIQUES

5

THE SQUAT

THE SQUAT IS OFTEN REFERRED TO AS THE "KING OF all exercises" due to its ability to engage multiple muscle groups and its effectiveness in building strength, power, and endurance. This chapter delves into the mechanics of the squat, explores various squat variations, highlights common errors and their corrections, and provides guidance on programming squats into your routine.

THE MECHANICS OF THE SQUAT

The squat is a compound movement that primarily targets the lower body, including the quadriceps, hamstrings, glutes, and calves. It also engages the core and back muscles to maintain stability throughout the movement.]

STEP-BY-STEP BREAKDOWN OF THE SQUAT

1. **Starting Position:** Stand with your feet shoulder-width apart, toes slightly turned out. The barbell should rest

on your upper traps (for a back squat) or on your front deltoids (for a front squat). Grip the bar tightly with your hands just outside shoulder width, and engage your core.

Squat

2. **Descending Phase:** Begin the movement by pushing your hips back, as if sitting into a chair. Keep your chest up, back straight, and knees tracking over your toes. Lower yourself until your thighs are at least parallel to the ground, ideally going as deep as your mobility allows while maintaining form.
3. **Ascending Phase:** Drive through your heels to push your body back up to the starting position. Focus on squeezing your glutes and keeping your core tight throughout the movement. Ensure your knees continue to track over your toes and avoid letting them cave inward.
4. **Breathing:** Inhale deeply as you lower into the squat and exhale as you rise. This breathing pattern helps maintain stability and power during the lift.

5. **Bracing:** Before you begin the descent, brace your core by taking a deep breath into your abdomen and holding it (this is similar to the Valsalva maneuver). This creates intra-abdominal pressure, stabilizing your spine during the lift.

VARIATIONS: BACK SQUAT, FRONT SQUAT, OVERHEAD SQUAT

Different squat variations can emphasize different muscle groups and challenge your body in unique ways. Each variation offers distinct benefits and can be incorporated into your routine to target specific goals.

Back Squat:

- **Positioning:** The barbell rests on the upper traps or across the rear deltoids. The back squat is the most common variation and is highly effective for building overall lower body strength.
- **Muscle Emphasis:** Primarily targets the quadriceps, hamstrings, and glutes, with significant engagement of the lower back and core for stability.
- *Technique Focus*: Maintain a neutral spine, keep your chest up, and ensure your knees track over your toes.

Front Squat:

- **Positioning:** The barbell is positioned on the front deltoids, with the elbows pointing forward. This variation places more emphasis on the quadriceps and upper back.
- **Muscle Emphasis:** Primarily targets the quadriceps and upper back, with reduced stress on the lower back compared to the back squat.

THE SQUAT

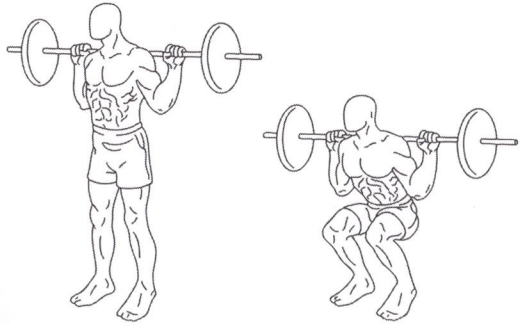

Back Squat

- **Technique Focus:** Keep your chest up and elbows high to maintain the barbell's position and avoid it rolling forward.

Front Squat

Overhead Squat:

- **Positioning:** The barbell is held overhead with arms fully extended, requiring significant shoulder stability and mobility.
- **Muscle Emphasis:** In addition to the lower body, the

overhead squat challenges the core, shoulders, and upper back.
- **Technique Focus:** Maintain a stable overhead position, keep your chest up, and ensure your knees track over your toes. This is a highly technical lift that requires good mobility and balance.

Overhead Squat

COMMON ERRORS AND CORRECTIONS

Even with the best intentions, common mistakes can occur during squats. Addressing these errors is crucial for optimizing performance and preventing injury.

Knee Valgus (Knees Caving In):

- **Error:** The knees collapse inward during the descent or ascent.
- **Correction:** Focus on pushing your knees outwards, ensuring they track over your toes. Strengthening the

glutes and abductors can help prevent this issue.

Butt Wink (Pelvic Tilt at the Bottom):

- **Error:** The lower back rounds at the bottom of the squat, known as a "butt wink."
- **Correction:** Improve hip mobility and strengthen the core to maintain a neutral spine throughout the movement. Avoid going deeper than your current mobility allows.

Leaning Forward:

- **Error:** Excessive forward lean during the squat, putting strain on the lower back.
- **Correction:** Focus on keeping your chest up and engaging your core. Widen your stance if necessary and ensure the barbell stays over the midfoot.

Rising Onto the Toes:

- **Error:** Heels lift off the ground during the squat, shifting weight onto the toes.
- **Correction:** Focus on driving through the heels and keeping your weight evenly distributed across your feet. Practice squatting with a heel wedge or weightlifting shoes if ankle mobility is an issue.

PROGRAMMING SQUATS INTO YOUR ROUTINE

Squats should be a staple in any strength training program, but how they're programmed depends on your goals and experience level.

Frequency: Depending on your training split, squats can be performed 2-3 times per week. Ensure there's adequate recovery between sessions to allow your muscles to repair and grow.

Repetition and Set Ranges:

- **Strength Focus:** For building maximal strength, perform 3-5 sets of 3-5 reps at a high intensity (85% or more of your 1RM).
- **Hypertrophy Focus:** For muscle growth, aim for 4-6 sets of 6-12 reps at a moderate intensity (65-75% of your 1RM).
- **Endurance Focus:** For muscular endurance, perform 3-4 sets of 12-20 reps at a lower intensity (50-65% of your 1RM).

Progressive Overload: To continue making progress, gradually increase the weight, reps, or sets over time. Ensure that you maintain proper form as you increase the load.

Accessory Work: Complement your squat training with accessory exercises that target weak points, such as lunges, step-ups, and leg presses. Strengthening the muscles involved in squats will lead to better performance and reduced injury risk.

Integrating squats into your routine will not only build strength and muscle but also improve overall athletic performance. By mastering the mechanics, addressing common errors, and programming squats effectively, you'll set yourself up for long-term success in your weight-lifting journey.

6

THE DEADLIFT

THE DEADLIFT IS A FUNDAMENTAL LIFT IN WEIGHT training, revered for its ability to build overall strength, power, and muscle mass. It is one of the most effective exercises for developing the posterior chain, including the hamstrings, glutes, lower back, and traps. This chapter explores the mechanics of the deadlift, various deadlift variations, common errors and their corrections, and offers guidance on how to program deadlifts into your routine for optimal results.

THE MECHANICS OF THE DEADLIFT

The deadlift is a compound movement that involves lifting a loaded barbell from the ground to a standing position. It engages multiple muscle groups and requires proper form to maximize effectiveness and prevent injury.

OLYMPIC SERIES: WEIGHT LIFTING

Deadlift

Step-by-Step Breakdown of the Deadlift:

1. **Starting Position:**
    - Stand with your feet hip-width apart, with the barbell positioned over the middle of your feet. Your shins should be close to the bar, almost touching it.
    - Grip the bar with a mixed grip (one hand overhand, the other underhand) or a double overhand grip, slightly wider than shoulder-width.
    - Hinge at the hips to lower your torso, keeping your back straight and your chest up. Your hips should be slightly higher than your knees.

2. **Pulling Phase:**
    - Engage your core and pull the bar upward by driving through your heels, extending your hips and knees simultaneously.
    - Keep the bar close to your body as you lift it,

ensuring that your back remains straight and your shoulders stay slightly ahead of the bar until it passes your knees.
- As the bar clears your knees, thrust your hips forward to fully extend your body and lock out at the top.

3. **Lockout Position:**
   - At the top of the lift, stand tall with your chest out, shoulders back, and hips fully extended. Avoid leaning back excessively.
   - Hold the position briefly before beginning the descent.

4. **Descending Phase:**
   - Initiate the descent by pushing your hips back and allowing the bar to lower along the same path it was lifted. Maintain a straight back and keep the bar close to your body.
   - Once the bar passes your knees, bend your knees to lower the bar to the ground in a controlled manner.

5. **Breathing and Bracing:**
   - Inhale deeply before lifting the bar, and exhale as you reach the lockout position. Bracing your core by creating intra-abdominal pressure is crucial for protecting your spine during the lift.

Deadlift illustration

VARIATIONS: CONVENTIONAL, SUMO, ROMANIAN DEADLIFT

Different deadlift variations can target specific muscle groups more intensively and accommodate different body types or goals. Here are three popular variations:

Conventional Deadlift:

Conventional Deadlift

THE DEADLIFT

- **Positioning:** Feet are hip-width apart, with hands gripping the bar just outside the legs. This is the most common form of deadlift, focusing on overall strength development.
- **Muscle Emphasis:** Primarily targets the hamstrings, glutes, lower back, and traps.
- *Technique Focus*: Ensure a straight back, engage the core, and drive through the heels.

Sumo Deadlift:

Sumo Deadlift

- **Positioning:** Feet are placed wider than shoulder-width, with toes pointed outward. Hands grip the bar inside the legs. This variation reduces the range of motion and shifts more emphasis onto the quadriceps and inner thighs.
- **Muscle Emphasis:** Targets the quadriceps, glutes, and adductors while reducing strain on the lower back.
- **Technique Focus:** Maintain an upright torso, push the knees out, and focus on driving through the heels.

Romanian Deadlift:

Romanian Deadlift

- **Positioning:** This variation starts from a standing position, with the barbell held at hip level. The movement focuses on hinging at the hips, lowering the bar along the legs while keeping them relatively straight.
- **Muscle Emphasis:** Primarily targets the hamstrings and glutes with less emphasis on the lower back.
- **Technique Focus:** Keep the legs slightly bent, push the hips back, and lower the bar with control, maintaining a straight back.

COMMON ERRORS AND CORRECTIONS

The deadlift, while highly effective, can lead to injuries if performed incorrectly. Understanding common errors and how to correct them is vital for safe and effective training.

Rounded Back:

- **Error:** Allowing the back to round during the lift, especially during the pulling phase, increases the risk of spinal injury.
- **Correction:** Focus on maintaining a neutral spine throughout the lift. Engage your core, and keep your chest up and shoulders back. Reducing the weight and perfecting your form with lighter loads can help correct this issue.

Hips Rising Too Quickly:

- **Error:** The hips rise faster than the chest during the lift, causing the lift to become more of a stiff-legged deadlift.
- **Correction:** Ensure that your hips and chest rise simultaneously by engaging your glutes and hamstrings at the start of the lift. Practice with a lighter weight to reinforce the correct movement pattern.

Barbell Too Far from the Body:

- **Error:** The bar drifts away from the body during the lift, placing unnecessary stress on the lower back.
- **Correction:** Keep the bar as close to your body as possible, almost grazing your shins on the way up. This ensures the load is distributed correctly and minimizes strain on the back.

Locking Out with an Overarched Back:

- **Error:** Leaning back excessively at the top of the lift, which can place undue stress on the lower back.
- **Correction:** Stand tall at the top of the lift without

hyperextending the spine. Focus on squeezing the glutes and maintaining a neutral spine throughout the lockout.

PROGRAMMING DEADLIFTS INTO YOUR ROUTINE

Deadlifts are a powerful tool in your training arsenal, but they need to be programmed carefully to avoid overtraining and ensure consistent progress.

Frequency: Depending on your goals and recovery ability, deadlifts can be performed 1-2 times per week. Given the intensity of the lift, sufficient recovery time between sessions is crucial.

Repetition and Set Ranges:

- **Strength Focus:** For maximal strength, perform 3-5 sets of 3-5 reps at a high intensity (85% or more of your 1RM). Focus on maintaining perfect form, especially as the weight increases.
- **Hypertrophy Focus:** For muscle growth, aim for 4-6 sets of 6-10 reps at a moderate intensity (65-75% of your 1RM). This range allows for sufficient volume to stimulate muscle growth while still challenging your strength.
- **Endurance Focus:** For muscular endurance, perform 3-4 sets of 12-15 reps at a lower intensity (50-65% of your 1RM). This can be particularly useful for conditioning phases or for athletes looking to improve their stamina.

Progressive Overload: As with any exercise, gradually increase the weight, reps, or sets over time to continue making progress. However, always prioritize form over the amount of weight lifted.

Accessory Work: Strengthen the muscles involved in the deadlift with accessory exercises like hamstring curls, glute bridges, and back extensions. These exercises can help address weaknesses and improve your deadlift performance.

Incorporating deadlifts into your routine will build foundational strength, enhance muscle mass, and improve overall athleticism. By mastering the mechanics, avoiding common errors, and programming deadlifts effectively, you'll set yourself up for continued success in your weight-lifting journey.

7

THE BENCH PRESS

THE BENCH PRESS IS ONE OF THE MOST ICONIC exercises in weight-lifting, often seen as a true measure of upper body strength. It's a compound movement that primarily targets the chest, triceps, and shoulders, and it forms a key component of many strength-training programs. This chapter delves into the mechanics of the bench press, explores its variations, highlights common errors, and discusses how to effectively program it into your routine.

THE MECHANICS OF THE BENCH PRESS

Understanding the correct mechanics of the bench press is crucial for maximizing your strength gains and minimizing the risk of injury. Here's a breakdown of the key steps involved in performing a standard bench press:

1. **Setup:** Begin by lying flat on a bench with your eyes directly under the barbell. Your feet should be flat on the ground, and your back should maintain its natural arch, with your shoulder blades pinched together. Grip

the bar slightly wider than shoulder-width apart, with your hands evenly spaced. A good reference is to align your pinky fingers with the rings on the barbell.
2. **Unrack the Bar:** Engage your core and take a deep breath before unracking the bar. Extend your arms to lift the bar off the rack, positioning it directly above your shoulders with your elbows locked out.
3. **Lower the Bar:** Begin the eccentric phase by slowly lowering the bar to your chest. Your elbows should be at about a 45-degree angle to your body, not flared out completely. Lower the bar in a controlled manner until it lightly touches the middle of your chest, roughly at the level of your sternum.
4. **Press the Bar Up:** After pausing briefly at the bottom, drive the bar upward by extending your arms. Exhale as you push the bar back to the starting position, keeping your elbows in line with your wrists. Ensure the bar moves in a straight line or slightly towards your face.
5. **Lock Out:** Once the barbell is fully extended, lock your elbows out while maintaining tension in your upper body. This completes one rep.

VARIATIONS: INCLINE, DECLINE, CLOSE-GRIP BENCH PRESS

While the standard bench press is highly effective, incorporating variations can target different muscle groups and add diversity to your training. Here are three popular bench press variations:

- **Incline Bench Press:** The incline bench press targets the upper portion of the pectoral muscles more than the standard flat bench press. To perform this variation, adjust the bench to an incline angle of about 30-45 degrees. The mechanics are similar to the flat bench press, but the incline shifts the emphasis to the upper chest and anterior deltoids.

Incline Bench Press

- **Decline Bench Press:** In contrast, the decline bench press emphasizes the lower part of the chest. Set the bench to a decline angle of about 15-30 degrees. The decline position reduces the range of motion and shifts more load onto the lower pectorals and triceps, making it a useful variation for overall chest development.

Decline Bench Press

- **Close-Grip Bench Press:** The close-grip bench press is a variation that focuses on the triceps. To perform this lift, grip the barbell with your hands closer together, typically shoulder-width apart. The closer grip increases triceps activation while also engaging the inner chest muscles. This variation is particularly effective for building triceps strength and lockout power.

Close-Grip Bench Pres

COMMON ERRORS AND CORRECTIONS

Even experienced lifters can fall into bad habits when it comes to the bench press. Here are some common mistakes and how to correct them:

- **Flaring the Elbows:** One of the most common mistakes is flaring the elbows out to 90 degrees, which puts excessive strain on the shoulders and increases the risk of injury. To correct this, tuck your elbows in slightly so they're at about a 45-degree angle to your body during the descent.
- **Bouncing the Bar Off the Chest:** Some lifters use momentum by bouncing the bar off their chest to help push the weight up. This not only reduces the effectiveness of the exercise but also increases the risk of injury to the sternum. To avoid this, focus on lowering the bar with control and pausing briefly before pressing it back up.
- **Arching the Lower Back Excessively:** While a slight arch in the lower back is natural and helps with stability, excessive arching can put unnecessary strain on the lumbar spine. Ensure that your lower back maintains a natural arch and that your glutes remain in contact with the bench throughout the lift.
- **Improper Foot Placement:** Many lifters neglect proper foot placement, which is crucial for generating power and stability during the bench press. Your feet should be flat on the floor, with your legs driving into the ground to create a stable base. Avoid lifting your feet off the ground or placing them on the bench.
- **Not Engaging the Lats:** The latissimus dorsi (lats) play a supportive role in the bench press, helping to stabilize the shoulders. Failing to engage the lats can reduce stability and increase the risk of shoulder injuries. To correct this, focus on pulling your shoulder blades together and down towards your hips as you lower the bar.

PROGRAMMING BENCH PRESS INTO YOUR ROUTINE

To make the most of the bench press, it's important to program it effectively into your workout routine. Here are some guidelines:

- **Frequency:** Depending on your goals, the bench press can be performed 1-3 times per week. For strength gains, consider incorporating it into a full-body or upper-body workout. If hypertrophy is the goal, higher volume with varied rep ranges can be beneficial.
- **Reps and Sets:** For strength, aim for 3-5 sets of 3-5 reps with heavier weights. For muscle growth, 3-4 sets of 8-12 reps with moderate weights is more effective. Adjust the weight and volume according to your goals and experience level.
- **Complementary Exercises:** To maximize chest development, pair the bench press with complementary exercises like dumbbell flyes, push-ups, and dips. These exercises target different angles of the chest and help balance out your upper-body training.
- **Progression:** Progressive overload is key to making gains in the bench press. Gradually increase the weight you lift, the number of sets, or the intensity of your workouts over time to continue making progress.
- **Recovery:** Allow sufficient time for recovery between bench press sessions. This might mean at least 48 hours of rest before working the same muscle group again, depending on the intensity of your workout.

Integrating the bench press into your training regimen with proper technique and variation will help you build strength, improve muscle definition, and achieve your fitness goals.

8

THE OVERHEAD PRESS

THE OVERHEAD PRESS, ALSO KNOWN AS THE shoulder press, is a fundamental exercise for building upper body strength and developing the shoulders. This compound movement targets the deltoids, triceps, and upper chest, and it's essential for anyone looking to build a strong, balanced physique. In this chapter, we'll explore the mechanics of the overhead press, examine its variations, address common errors, and discuss how to program it effectively into your routine.

THE MECHANICS OF THE OVERHEAD PRESS

The overhead press is a relatively simple yet challenging movement that requires proper form to maximize its benefits and prevent injury. Here's a step-by-step guide to performing a standing overhead press:

1. **Setup:** Stand with your feet shoulder-width apart, and grasp the barbell with a grip slightly wider than shoulder-width. Your hands should be just outside your shoulders

when the bar is resting on your upper chest. The barbell should start at about collarbone height, with your elbows slightly in front of the bar, not directly under it.
2. **Bracing:** Before initiating the lift, engage your core by taking a deep breath and tightening your abdominal muscles. Your glutes should be squeezed, and your rib cage should be down to prevent excessive arching of the lower back. This bracing helps stabilize your torso during the press.
3. **Pressing the Bar:** Begin the press by driving the barbell upward in a straight line. As the bar passes your forehead, slightly tilt your head back to allow the bar to clear. Once the bar passes your head, push your head forward under the bar, ensuring the barbell stays in line with your midline. Fully extend your arms overhead, locking out your elbows at the top.
4. **Lowering the Bar:** Lower the bar back down to your starting position with control, keeping your core engaged. The bar should follow the same path down as it did up, staying close to your body.
5. **Breathing:** Exhale as you press the bar overhead, and inhale as you lower it back down. Consistent breathing helps maintain rhythm and control throughout the movement.

VARIATIONS: STANDING, SEATED, PUSH PRESS

While the standing overhead press is the most common form, there are several variations that can target different aspects of shoulder strength and stability:

- **Standing Overhead Press:** This is the standard version

of the lift and is performed while standing. It engages the entire body, requiring core stability and leg drive to maintain balance. The standing press is excellent for building overall strength and coordination.
- **Seated Overhead Press:** The seated version isolates the shoulders more by removing the legs and core from the equation. Sitting on a bench with back support, the seated press allows you to focus entirely on the shoulder muscles. This variation is useful for targeting the deltoids but doesn't engage the stabilizing muscles as much as the standing press.
- **Push Press:** The push press is a dynamic variation that involves a slight dip of the knees and hips before explosively pressing the bar overhead. This movement allows you to lift heavier weights than you could with a strict press, as the leg drive helps initiate the movement. The push press is excellent for developing power and strength, particularly in the upper body.

COMMON ERRORS AND CORRECTIONS

The overhead press is a straightforward movement, but several common mistakes can hinder your progress and increase the risk of injury. Here's how to avoid them:
- **Overarching the Lower Back:** Excessive arching of the lower back, known as hyperextension, is a common error in the overhead press. This can put undue stress on the lumbar spine and lead to injury. To correct this, focus on bracing your core and glutes throughout the movement. Keep your rib cage down and avoid leaning back excessively during the press.

- **Flaring the Elbows:** Allowing the elbows to flare out too much can reduce the effectiveness of the press and strain the shoulder joints. To avoid this, keep your elbows slightly in front of the barbell throughout the movement. This ensures that the bar stays in a straight path and reduces shoulder strain.
- **Not Engaging the Core:** A weak or unengaged core can lead to instability during the press, making it harder to lift the bar and increasing the risk of losing balance. Always engage your core by tightening your abdominal muscles before starting the lift. This provides a stable base and supports the spine during the press.
- **Using Too Much Leg Drive:** In the strict overhead press, using excessive leg drive is a form of cheating and can prevent you from fully developing your shoulder strength. If you find yourself relying on leg drive, consider reducing the weight and focusing on strict form. Save the leg drive for the push press variation.
- **Inconsistent Bar Path:** The barbell should move in a straight line or slightly backward as you press it overhead. If the bar moves forward or follows an inconsistent path, it can throw off your balance and reduce the efficiency of the lift. Focus on driving the bar straight up and keeping it close to your face and body.

PROGRAMMING OVERHEAD PRESS INTO YOUR ROUTINE

The overhead press is a versatile exercise that can be incorporated into various training programs, whether your goal is strength, hypertrophy, or overall fitness. Here are some tips for programming it effectively:

- **Frequency:** Depending on your goals and overall program, the overhead press can be performed 1-2 times per week. It can be part of an upper-body day or included in a full-body workout.
- **Reps and Sets:** For strength, aim for 3-5 sets of 3-6 reps with heavy weights. For muscle growth, 3-4 sets of 8-12 reps with moderate weights can be more effective. Adjust the volume and intensity based on your goals and how the press fits into your overall routine.
- **Complementary Exercises:** To fully develop the shoulders and upper body, pair the overhead press with complementary exercises like lateral raises, face pulls, and triceps extensions. These exercises help target the smaller shoulder muscles and improve overall shoulder health.
- **Progression:** Like any lift, progressive overload is key to making gains in the overhead press. Gradually increase the weight, volume, or intensity of your presses over time. Tracking your progress and making small, consistent improvements is essential for long-term success.
- **Recovery**: The shoulders can be prone to overuse injuries, so it's important to allow adequate recovery between overhead press sessions. Ensure you have at least 48 hours of rest between sessions that heavily involve the shoulders.

By mastering the mechanics of the overhead press, exploring its variations, and programming it effectively, you can build strong, powerful shoulders and enhance your overall upper body strength. Whether you're training for strength, muscle growth, or athletic performance, the overhead press is an invaluable exercise in your routine.

SECTION THREE

ADVANCED TECHNIQUES AND TRAINING

9

ACCESSORY LIFTS AND THEIR ROLE

IN WEIGHT-LIFTING, ACCESSORY LIFTS PLAY A CRUCIAL role in supporting and enhancing the performance of main compound exercises. While compound lifts like the squat, bench press, and deadlift form the foundation of strength training, accessory lifts target specific muscle groups and help address weaknesses, improve imbalances, and contribute to overall strength and hypertrophy. This chapter explores the importance of accessory lifts, highlights key exercises for major muscle groups, and offers guidance on balancing them with main lifts and incorporating isolation exercises.

THE IMPORTANCE OF ACCESSORY LIFTS IN BUILDING STRENGTH

Accessory lifts are exercises that complement and enhance the effectiveness of primary compound lifts. They are designed to target specific muscles or muscle groups that are either involved in the main lifts or that support them indirectly. Here's why accessory lifts are essential in a well-rounded strength training program:

1. **Addressing Weak Points:** Accessory lifts help address weaknesses or imbalances in specific muscle groups that might limit performance in compound lifts. For example, if your triceps are weaker, it can hinder your bench press performance. Accessory exercises like triceps dips or extensions can help strengthen these muscles.
2. **Enhancing Muscle Development:** While compound lifts target multiple muscles simultaneously, accessory lifts allow for more focused work on individual muscles. This targeted approach helps promote balanced muscle development and can contribute to greater overall hypertrophy.
3. **Improving Technique and Stability:** Some accessory lifts focus on improving the stability and technique of main lifts. For instance, exercises like planks and stability ball rollouts strengthen the core, which is crucial for maintaining proper form during heavy squats or deadlifts.
4. **Reducing Injury Risk:** By strengthening smaller stabilizing muscles and improving joint stability, accessory lifts can help reduce the risk of injury. This preventative aspect is especially important for maintaining long-term progress and overall health.
5. **Enhancing Recovery:** Accessory work can also play a role in recovery by increasing blood flow to the muscles, promoting better circulation, and aiding in the prevention of stiffness and soreness.

KEY ACCESSORY LIFTS FOR EACH MAJOR MUSCLE GROUP

To build a balanced and strong physique, it's important to incorporate accessory lifts that target each major muscle group. Here's a breakdown of effective accessory lifts for different areas of the body:

- **Chest:**
    - *Dumbbell Flyes*: Focuses on the pectoral muscles, providing a full range of motion and enhancing muscle stretch.
    - *Cable Crossovers*: Targets the inner chest and helps with muscle definition.
    - *Incline Dumbbell Press*: Emphasizes the upper chest, complementing the flat bench press.

Dumbbell Flyes

ACCESSORY LIFTS AND THEIR ROLE

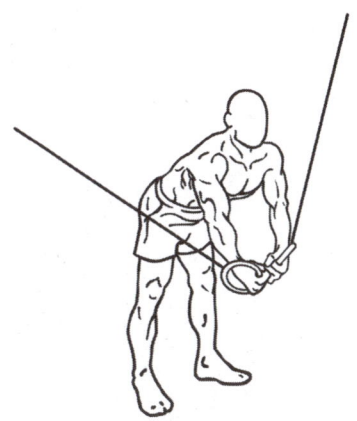

Cable Crossover

Incline Dumbbell Press

- **Back:**
  - *Lat Pulldowns*: A great exercise for developing the latissimus dorsi and improving the width of the back.
  - *Seated Rows*: Targets the middle back and helps with overall back thickness.
  - *Face Pulls*: Focuses on the rear deltoids and upper back, improving posture and shoulder health.

Lat Pulldown

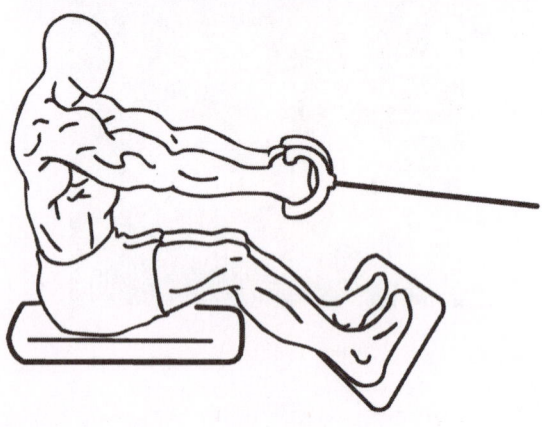

Seated Row

- **Shoulders:**
  - *Lateral Raises*: Isolates the lateral delt*oids, helping to build width and definition in the shoulders.*
  - *Rear Delt Flyes: Targets the posterior deltoids and*

helps with overall shoulder balance.
- *Front Raises: Emphasizes the anterior delt*oids and complements pressing movements.

Lateral Raises

Front Raises

- **Legs:**
    - Leg Curls: Focuses on the hamstrings, balancing the quadriceps work from squats and leg presses.
    - *Leg Extensions: Isolates the quadriceps, enhancing overall leg development.*
    - *Bulgarian Split Squats: Targets the quads and glutes while improving single-leg strength and stability.*

Leg Curls

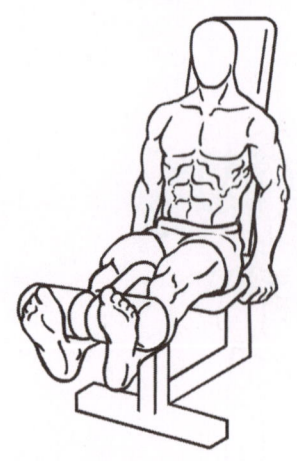

Leg Extensions

ACCESSORY LIFTS AND THEIR ROLE

Bulgarian Split Squat

- **Arms:**
    - Bicep Curls: Various forms (e.g., barbell, dumbbell, hammer curls) to target the biceps from different angles.
    - Triceps Extensions: Includes overhead and skull crushers to effectively target the triceps.
    - *Cable Pushdowns: Focuses on the triceps, providing constant tension throughout the range of motio*n.

Bicep Curls

OLYMPIC SERIES: WEIGHT LIFTING

Standing triceps extension

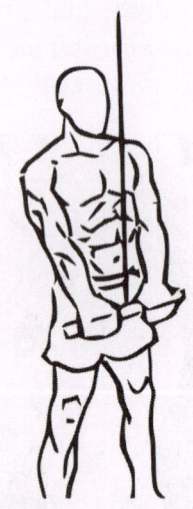

Triceps pushdown with cable

ACCESSORY LIFTS AND THEIR ROLE

- **Core:**
  - *Hanging Leg Raises: Strengthens the lower abs and improves core stability.*
  - *Russian Twists: Targets the obliques and enhances rotational strength.*
  - *Ab Rollouts: Engages the entire core and challenges stability.*

Hanging Leg Raises

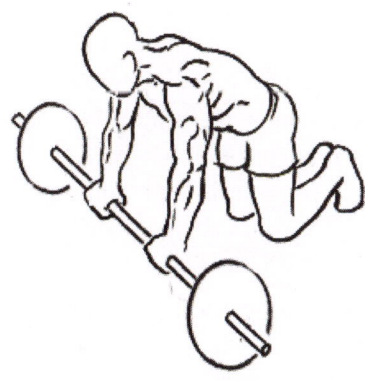

Ab Rollout

BALANCING MAIN LIFTS WITH ACCESSORY WORK

Effectively integrating accessory lifts into your routine requires a balance with main compound lifts to ensure a comprehensive and effective training program. Here's how to achieve this balance:

1. **Prioritize Compound Lifts:** Compound lifts should be the cornerstone of your routine, performed early in the workout when you're freshest. They are key for building overall strength and muscle mass.
2. **Incorporate Accessory Work Strategically:** Accessory lifts should complement the main lifts. Perform them after your primary exercises to address specific weaknesses or imbalances. This approach ensures that you're not fatigued before your most important lifts.
3. **Adjust Volume and Intensity:** Accessory lifts generally involve higher repetitions and lower weights compared to compound lifts. This helps in focusing on muscle endurance and hypertrophy without compromising your ability to perform heavy compound lifts.
4. **Monitor Recovery:** Be mindful of the total training volume and recovery needs. Too much accessory work can lead to overtraining or interfere with recovery. Ensure that your overall program allows for adequate rest and recovery between sessions.
5. **Variety and Adaptation:** Regularly vary your accessory lifts to avoid plateaus and keep your training engaging. This could involve changing exercises, adjusting rep ranges, or incorporating different training techniques like supersets or drop sets.

INCORPORATING ISOLATION EXERCISES

Isolation exercises target specific muscles without significantly involving other muscle groups. They are particularly useful for improving muscle definition and addressing weak points. Here's how to effectively incorporate isolation exercises into your routine:

1. **Focus on Weak Areas:** Use isolation exercises to target and strengthen weak or underdeveloped muscles that may be limiting your performance in compound lifts.
2. **Enhance Muscle Definition:** Isolation exercises are excellent for achieving muscle definition and aesthetic goals. Incorporate them towards the end of your workout to fully fatigue specific muscle groups.
3. **Incorporate Mind-Muscle Connection:** Isolation exercises allow for greater focus on the muscle being worked. Pay attention to the mind-muscle connection by consciously contracting the target muscle throughout the movement.
4. **Use Progressive Overload:** Just like with compound lifts, apply progressive overload principles to isolation exercises by gradually increasing weight, reps, or intensity over time.
5. **Integrate with Compound Lifts:** While isolation exercises are valuable, they should complement—not replace—compound lifts. Ensure that your routine balances both types of exercises to achieve overall strength and muscle development.

By understanding the role of accessory lifts and incorporating them effectively into your training program, you can enhance your overall performance, address specific weaknesses, and achieve a balanced and well-developed physique. Whether you're aiming for strength, hypertrophy, or overall fitness, accessory work plays a crucial role in reaching your goals and optimizing your results.

10

ADVANCED LIFTING TECHNIQUES

A S YOU PROGRESS IN YOUR WEIGHT-LIFTING journey, incorporating advanced lifting techniques can provide new challenges, enhance muscle growth, and break through plateaus. These techniques involve manipulating various training variables to optimize your performance and results. This chapter delves into advanced lifting methods, including tempo and time under tension, drop sets, supersets, pyramid sets, chains and bands for resistance, and the conjugate method with periodization techniques.

INCORPORATING TEMPO AND TIME UNDER TENSION

Tempo refers to the speed at which you perform each phase of a lift, and time under tension (TUT) is the total duration your muscles are under strain during an exercise. Manipulating tempo and TUT can significantly impact muscle growth and strength development.

1. **Understanding Tempo:** Tempo is usually expressed in a series of four numbers, representing the duration of the eccentric (lowering), isometric (pause), concentric (lifting), and second isometric phases. For example, a tempo of 3-1-1-0 means three seconds for the eccentric phase, one-second pause, one-second concentric phase, and no pause at the top.
2. **Time Under Tension (TUT):** TUT is the total time your muscles are engaged during an exercise. Increasing TUT can lead to greater muscle hypertrophy because the muscles are under continuous strain. For instance, performing slow and controlled reps increases TUT, enhancing muscle fatigue and growth.
3. **Applications:** To incorporate tempo and TUT, you might perform slow, controlled reps for exercises like squats or bench presses, focusing on maintaining tension throughout the lift. For example, lowering the barbell over five seconds and pausing briefly at the bottom before pressing up can create a significant training effect.

THE ROLE OF DROP SETS, SUPERSETS, AND PYRAMID SETS

Advanced training techniques like drop sets, supersets, and pyramid sets are designed to push your muscles beyond their usual limits and promote increased strength and hypertrophy.
1. **Drop Sets:** A drop set involves performing a set of an exercise to failure, then immediately reducing the weight and continuing the exercise until failure again.

This technique maximizes muscle fatigue and stimulates growth by extending the set beyond normal limits. For example, you might start with a heavy weight for bicep curls, drop to a lighter weight, and continue curling until you reach failure.

2. **Supersets:** Supersets involve performing two exercises back-to-back with little to no rest between them. Supersets can be categorized into two types:
    - *Antagonistic Supersets*: Involve exercises targeting opposing muscle groups, such as biceps and triceps. This method allows one muscle group to recover while the other is being worked.
    - *Agonistic Supersets*: Involve exercises targeting the same muscle group, such as chest presses followed by chest flyes. This method increases muscle fatigue and intensity.

3. **Pyramid Sets:** Pyramid sets involve adjusting the weight and repetitions for each set in a progressive or reverse manner. In a traditional pyramid set, you start with lighter weights and higher reps, then gradually increase the weight and decrease the reps. This method helps in building both strength and endurance.
    - *Ascending Pyramid*: Start with lighter weights and higher reps, progressively increasing the weight and decreasing the reps with each set.
    - *Descending Pyramid*: Begin with heavy weights and low reps, then decrease the weight and increase the reps for each subsequent set.

UTILIZING CHAINS AND BANDS FOR RESISTANCE

Chains and bands add variable resistance to exercises, providing unique benefits that standard weights cannot. They are used to enhance strength, power, and muscle activation.

1. **Chains:** Chains increase resistance as they lift off the ground during an exercise. As you lift the barbell, more chain links come off the floor, progressively increasing the weight. Chains help to improve strength throughout the entire range of motion and promote explosive power.
   - *Application*: Attach chains to the barbell during squats or bench presses. The resistance increases as you lift the bar, challenging your muscles to work harder during the most challenging part of the lift.
2. **Bands:** Bands provide accommodating resistance, meaning the resistance increases as the band stretches. They are particularly useful for developing explosive strength and improving lockout power.
   - *Application*: Use bands in conjunction with barbells for exercises like squats or deadlifts. The bands add resistance at the top of the lift, which enhances muscle activation and strengthens the lockout phase.

CONJUGATE METHOD AND PERIODIZATION TECHNIQUES

The conjugate method and periodization are advanced training techniques used to enhance performance and prevent plateaus by systematically varying training variables.

1. **Conjugate Method:** Developed by Louie Simmons and popularized by Westside Barbell, the conjugate method involves rotating different training focuses each week, such as maximal effort, dynamic effort, and repetition effort. This approach prevents stagnation and ensures balanced development of strength, speed, and endurance.
    - *Maximal Effort*: Focuses on lifting the heaviest possible weights for low reps to develop maximal strength.
    - *Dynamic Effort*: Emphasizes speed and explosive power by lifting lighter weights at a fast pace.
    - *Repetition Effort*: Concentrates on muscle hypertrophy and endurance through higher rep ranges with moderate weights.
2. **Periodization Techniques:** Periodization involves structuring training into distinct phases or cycles to optimize performance and recovery. The most common periodization models include:
    - *Linear Periodization*: Gradually increases intensity and decreases volume over time. Typically starts with high volume and low intensity and progresses to lower volume and higher intensity.
    - *Undulating Periodization*: Varies intensity and volume within a week or training cycle, offering greater variation and preventing adaptation. For example, you might alternate between high-rep days and low-rep, heavy weight days.
    - *Block Periodization*: Divides training into specific blocks or phases, each focusing on a particular training goal such as strength, hypertrophy, or

power. Each phase builds upon the previous one, leading to overall progress and peak performance.

INTEGRATING ADVANCED TECHNIQUES

To effectively integrate advanced lifting techniques into your routine:
- **Start Gradually:** Introduce one or two advanced techniques at a time to gauge their impact on your training and recovery.
- **Monitor Progress:** Track your performance and muscle development to assess the effectiveness of the techniques and make adjustments as needed.
- **Ensure Recovery:** Advanced techniques can increase training intensity and volume, so ensure adequate recovery time between workouts to avoid overtraining.
- **Consult Professionals:** If you're new to advanced techniques, consider seeking guidance from a qualified trainer or coach to ensure proper execution and avoid injury.

By incorporating these advanced lifting techniques into your training regimen, you can enhance your strength, muscle growth, and overall performance. These methods provide variety and challenge, helping you continue progressing and achieving your fitness goals.

11

PROGRAMMING FOR STRENGTH AND HYPERTROPHY

CREATING AN EFFECTIVE WEIGHT-LIFTING PROGRAM requires a thoughtful approach to ensure that both strength and hypertrophy goals are met. This chapter will guide you through the fundamentals of periodization, developing a customized weight-lifting program, integrating deloading and recovery weeks, and the importance of tracking progress and adjusting your program.

UNDERSTANDING PERIODIZATION: LINEAR VS. NON-LINEAR

Periodization is the systematic planning of training to optimize performance and achieve specific goals. It involves structuring your training program into phases or cycles to prevent stagnation and enhance progress. There are two primary types of periodization: linear and non-linear.

1. **Linear Periodization:**
    - *Concept*: Linear periodization involves gradually

increasing the intensity of your workouts while decreasing the volume over time. This model is straightforward and often used by beginners.
- *Phases*: Typically, a linear periodization program starts with high volume and low intensity (e.g., more sets and reps with lighter weights) and progressively shifts to lower volume and higher intensity (e.g., fewer sets and reps with heavier weights).
- *Example*: A 12-week linear periodization program might start with 4 weeks of 3 sets of 12 reps at 70% of your one-rep max (1RM), followed by 4 weeks of 4 sets of 8 reps at 80% 1RM, and concluding with 4 weeks of 5 sets of 5 reps at 85% 1RM.

2. **Non-Linear (Undulating) Periodization:**
   - *Concept*: Non-linear periodization, or undulating periodization, involves varying the intensity and volume on a more frequent basis, such as weekly or daily. This model is more flexible and can prevent adaptation and plateauing.
   - *Phases*: In non-linear periodization, different training focuses are cycled more frequently. For instance, one week might emphasize strength with heavy weights and low reps, while the next week focuses on hypertrophy with moderate weights and higher reps.
   - *Example*: A 4-week non-linear periodization program could include strength-focused workouts (e.g., 4 sets of 4 reps at 85% 1RM) followed by hypertrophy-focused workouts (e.g., 3 sets of 12 reps at 70% 1RM) in alternating weeks.

BUILDING A CUSTOMIZED WEIGHT-LIFTING PROGRAM

Designing a personalized weight-lifting program involves considering your specific goals, current fitness level, and available resources. Here's how to build a program tailored to your needs:

1. **Set Clear Goals:** Determine whether your primary focus is strength, hypertrophy, endurance, or a combination of these. Your goals will influence the structure and content of your program.
   - *Strength*: Emphasizes heavy weights and low reps to increase maximal force production.
   - *Hypertrophy*: Focuses on moderate to heavy weights with moderate reps to promote muscle growth.
   - *Endurance*: Incorporates lighter weights with higher reps to enhance muscular stamina.
2. **Choose the Right Exercises:** Select exercises that align with your goals and cover all major muscle groups. Include a mix of compound and isolation exercises.
   - *Compound Exercises*: Squats, deadlifts, bench presses, and pull-ups engage multiple muscle groups and are crucial for overall strength and muscle development.
   - *Isolation Exercises*: Bicep curls, triceps extensions, and calf raises target specific muscles for balanced development.
3. **Determine Volume and Intensity:** Based on your goals, decide on the appropriate volume (total sets and reps) and intensity (weight used). For strength, focus on lower reps (3-6) with higher weights (75-90% of

1RM). For hypertrophy, aim for moderate reps (8-12) with moderate weights (60-75% of 1RM).
4. **Structure Your Program:** Organize your weekly routine to include different training days and muscle group focuses.
    - *Example Split*: A common split might be a 4-day program with Upper Body (Day 1), Lower Body (Day 2), Rest (Day 3), Upper Body (Day 4), and Lower Body (Day 5), with two rest days.
5. **Include Warm-Ups and Cool-Downs:** Start each session with a dynamic warm-up to prepare your muscles and joints for the workout. End with a cool-down that includes stretching to promote recovery and flexibility.

DELOADING AND RECOVERY WEEKS

Deloading and recovery weeks are essential for preventing overtraining and ensuring long-term progress. These periods allow your body to recover and adapt, reducing the risk of injury and improving performance.

1. **Deloading:**
    - *Concept*: A deload week involves reducing the intensity and volume of your workouts to give your body a break. This helps to recover from accumulated fatigue and allows for better progress in subsequent training phases.
    - *Implementation*: During a deload week, you might reduce the weight lifted to 50-60% of your usual working weights, decrease the number of sets and reps, or reduce the frequency of workouts. For

example, if you normally lift 80% of your 1RM, you might reduce it to 60% during the deload week.
2. **Recovery Weeks:**
    - *Concept*: Recovery weeks involve complete rest or very light activity to allow for full recovery. This is particularly useful after intense training cycles or competitions.
    - *Implementation*: During a recovery week, you might engage in low-intensity activities like walking, light jogging, or yoga, or take a complete break from structured exercise. The focus is on active recovery and reducing overall training stress.

TRACKING PROGRESS AND ADJUSTING YOUR PROGRAM

Regularly tracking your progress and making adjustments to your program are vital for continued improvement and goal achievement.

1. **Track Key Metrics:**
    - *Strength Metrics*: Record your 1RM or estimated 1RM for major lifts and track improvements over time.
    - *Hypertrophy Metrics*: Monitor muscle size through measurements or progress photos, and note any increases in muscle definition or volume.
    - *Performance Metrics*: Track improvements in workout performance, such as increased weights, reps, or workout efficiency.
2. **Evaluate and Adjust:**
    - *Assess Progress*: Periodically review your progress

to determine if you're meeting your goals. Look for improvements in strength, muscle size, or other relevant metrics.
- *Adjust Program*: Based on your progress assessment, make necessary adjustments to your program. This might include increasing weights, changing exercises, modifying volume or intensity, or altering the periodization model.

3 **Listen to Your Body:**
- *Monitor Fatigue and Recovery:* Pay attention to signs of overtraining, such as persistent fatigue, soreness, or decreased performance. Adjust your program if you experience these symptoms to avoid injury and ensure optimal recovery.
- *Modify Goals*: As you progress, your goals may evolve. Update your program to reflect any new objectives or training priorities.

4. **Seek Feedback:** Consider consulting with a coach or trainer for professional feedback on your program and progress. They can provide valuable insights and help you make informed adjustments.

By understanding and implementing effective periodization strategies, building a customized weight-lifting program, incorporating deloading and recovery weeks, and tracking your progress, you can create a balanced and dynamic training regimen that fosters both strength and hypertrophy. This approach will help you achieve your fitness goals, optimize performance, and maintain long-term progress.

SECTION FOUR

NUTRITION AND RECOVERY

12

NUTRITION FOR WEIGHT-LIFTING

NUTRITION IS A CRITICAL COMPONENT OF ANY successful weight-lifting program. Proper dietary habits not only support muscle growth and strength development but also enhance recovery and overall performance. This chapter provides an in-depth look at the essential elements of nutrition for weight-lifting, including macronutrients, creating a diet for strength and muscle gain, pre- and post-workout nutrition, and effective supplementation.

MACRONUTRIENTS: PROTEIN, CARBS, AND FATS

Macronutrients—protein, carbohydrates, and fats—are fundamental to a well-rounded diet for weight-lifting. Each plays a unique role in supporting muscle growth, recovery, and overall energy levels.

1. **Protein:**
    - *Role*: Protein is essential for muscle repair, growth,

and recovery. It provides the building blocks (amino acids) needed to repair muscle fibers damaged during weight-lifting.
- *Sources*: High-quality protein sources include lean meats (chicken, beef, turkey), fish, eggs, dairy products (Greek yogurt, cottage cheese), and plant-based options (tofu, legumes, quinoa).
- *Recommended Intake*: Aim for 1.6 to 2.2 grams of protein per kilogram of body weight per day. This range supports muscle protein synthesis and recovery.

2. **Carbohydrates:**
   - *Role*: Carbohydrates are the primary source of energy for high-intensity workouts and help replenish glycogen stores in muscles and liver. They also support recovery by providing energy for muscle repair.
   - *Sources*: Include complex carbohydrates such as whole grains (brown rice, oats, quinoa), fruits, vegetables, and legumes. Simple carbohydrates (such as fruits or sports drinks) can be beneficial around workouts for quick energy.
   - *Recommended Intake*: Carbohydrate needs vary based on training intensity and volume but generally range from 4 to 7 grams per kilogram of body weight per day.

3. **Fats:**
   - *Role*: Fats are crucial for hormone production, including hormones like testosterone and estrogen, which play a role in muscle growth and recovery. They also provide a source of sustained energy.

- *Sources*: Opt for healthy fats from sources like avocados, nuts, seeds, olive oil, and fatty fish (salmon, mackerel).
- *Recommended Intake*: Aim for fats to comprise about 20-35% of your total daily caloric intake. Focus on unsaturated fats and limit saturated and trans fats.

BUILDING A DIET FOR STRENGTH AND MUSCLE GAIN

Designing a diet to support strength and muscle gain involves balancing macronutrients and ensuring adequate caloric intake. Here's how to structure your diet for optimal results:

1. **Calculate Caloric Needs:**
    - *Determine Maintenance Calories*: Calculate your total daily energy expenditure (TDEE) based on your basal metabolic rate (BMR) and activity level.
    - *Create a Caloric Surplus:* For muscle gain, aim for a caloric surplus of 250-500 calories per day above your TDEE. This surplus provides extra energy for muscle growth.
2. **Meal Timing:**
    - *Frequent Meals*: Consume 4-6 small to moderate-sized meals throughout the day to maintain energy levels and support muscle repair.
    - *Balance Macronutrients*: Ensure each meal includes a balance of protein, carbohydrates, and fats to support sustained energy and recovery.

NUTRITION FOR WEIGHT-LIFTING

3. **Hydration:**
   - *Importance*: Staying hydrated is vital for performance and recovery. Dehydration can impair strength, endurance, and muscle function.
   - *Recommendations*: Drink at least 8-10 glasses (2-3 liters) of water per day, and more if you are engaging in intense workouts or in hot climates. Consider adding electrolytes if sweating excessively.
4. **Meal Composition:**
   - *Pre-Workout*: Include a balanced meal 1-2 hours before your workout, focusing on complex carbohydrates and moderate protein. For example, a meal of oatmeal with protein powder and fruit.
   - *Post-Workout*: Aim for a meal or snack within 30-60 minutes after your workout, combining protein and carbohydrates to replenish glycogen stores and aid muscle recovery. Examples include a protein shake with a banana or a chicken breast with sweet potatoes.

PRE-WORKOUT AND POST-WORKOUT NUTRITION

Proper nutrition around your workouts can significantly impact performance and recovery. Here's a closer look at how to optimize pre- and post-workout nutrition:

1. **Pre-Workout Nutrition:**
   - *Timing*: Eat a balanced meal 1-2 hours before training or a smaller snack 30-60 minutes prior if you're short on time.
   - *Composition*: Focus on easily digestible

carbohydrates for energy and moderate protein to support muscle protein synthesis. Avoid high-fat or high-fiber foods immediately before working out, as they can cause discomfort.
  - *Example Pre-Workout Meals*: Whole grain toast with avocado and an egg, or Greek yogurt with berries and honey.
2. **Post-Workout Nutrition:**
  - *Timing*: Consume a post-workout meal or snack within 30-60 minutes to optimize recovery and muscle repair.
  - *Composition*: Include a mix of protein and carbohydrates to replenish glycogen stores and support muscle repair. Protein shakes, chocolate milk, or a balanced meal with lean protein and complex carbs are effective options.
  - *Example Post-Workout Meals:* A smoothie made with protein powder, spinach, banana, and almond milk, or grilled chicken with quinoa and steamed vegetables.

SUPPLEMENTATION: WHAT WORKS AND WHAT DOESN'T

Supplements can aid in achieving your weight-lifting goals, but it's important to understand which ones are effective and necessary for your individual needs.

1. **Effective Supplements:**
  - *Protein Powders*: Whey, casein, and plant-based protein powders can help meet daily protein needs and support muscle growth. Whey protein is particularly effective due to its fast absorption

and high leucine content.
- *Creatine Monohydrate*: Creatine enhances strength, power, and muscle mass by increasing phosphocreatine stores in muscles. It's one of the most researched and effective supplements for improving performance.
- *Branched-Chain Amino Acids (BCAAs)*: Leucine, isoleucine, and valine can help reduce muscle soreness and support muscle repair, although their benefits might be less significant if your overall protein intake is sufficient.
- *Beta-Alanine*: This supplement helps buffer lactic acid buildup, improving endurance and reducing fatigue during high-intensity exercise.

2. **Supplements with Limited Evidence:**
   - *Pre-Workout Blends*: Many pre-workout supplements contain stimulants like caffeine or beta-alanine, which can enhance focus and performance. However, their effectiveness can vary, and it's important to choose products with transparent labeling and minimal additives.
   - *Testosterone Boosters*: Claims about natural testosterone boosters are often exaggerated. While some ingredients may have a slight effect, they are generally less effective than proper diet and training.

3. **Supplements to Approach with Caution:**
   - *Fat Burners*: These supplements often contain stimulants or compounds that promise rapid fat loss but may have limited evidence supporting their effectiveness. Additionally, they can have adverse side effects.

- *Unverified Products*: Be cautious of supplements that make bold claims without scientific backing or are marketed as miracle solutions. Always research and choose supplements with proven efficacy and safety.
4. **Consultation:** Before starting any supplement regimen, it's advisable to consult with a healthcare provider or a registered dietitian to ensure that the supplements are appropriate for your individual health needs and fitness goals.

By understanding macronutrients, building a diet tailored to strength and muscle gain, optimizing pre- and post-workout nutrition, and making informed choices about supplementation, you can significantly enhance your weight-lifting performance and overall results. A well-rounded approach to nutrition not only supports muscle growth and recovery but also contributes to long-term health and fitness success.

13

THE IMPORTANCE OF RECOVERY

RECOVERY IS AN ESSENTIAL COMPONENT OF ANY weight-lifting program, playing a critical role in ensuring long-term success and preventing injury. Effective recovery allows the body to repair and adapt to the stresses of weight training, enhancing muscle growth, strength, and overall performance. This chapter explores various aspects of recovery, including the significance of sleep, active recovery techniques, managing fatigue and overtraining, and the benefits of massage and physiotherapy.

THE ROLE OF SLEEP IN MUSCLE RECOVERY

Sleep is a fundamental aspect of recovery that greatly influences muscle repair, growth, and overall well-being. During sleep, the body engages in essential processes that support physical recovery and performance enhancement.

1. **Muscle Repair and Growth:**
    - *Hormone Production*: During sleep, the body produces growth hormone, which is critical for

muscle repair and growth. This hormone stimulates protein synthesis, aiding in the repair of muscle fibers that have been stressed during weight-lifting. Adequate sleep ensures optimal levels of this hormone, supporting effective recovery and muscle development.

- *Protein Synthesis*: Sleep facilitates increased protein synthesis, which is vital for muscle repair and growth. The deeper stages of sleep are particularly important for this process. By promoting protein synthesis, sleep helps in the rebuilding and strengthening of muscles damaged during workouts.

2. **Sleep Duration and Quality:**
   - *Recommendations*: Aim for 7-9 hours of quality sleep each night. Consistent sleep patterns are crucial for maintaining overall health and maximizing recovery. Individual sleep needs can vary, but maintaining a regular sleep schedule is key to supporting muscle repair and performance.
   - *Sleep Quality*: Improving sleep quality involves creating a restful environment. This includes keeping your bedroom dark, cool, and quiet, and avoiding screens and stimulants before bedtime. Establishing a pre-sleep routine, such as reading or practicing relaxation techniques, can also enhance sleep quality.

3. **Impact of Sleep Deprivation:**
   - *Performance and Recovery*: Sleep deprivation can significantly impair physical performance, increase fatigue, and delay muscle recovery. Chronic lack of sleep can lead to decreased strength, endurance, and

overall fitness, as well as a heightened risk of injury. Ensuring adequate sleep is essential for maintaining optimal training performance and recovery.

ACTIVE RECOVERY TECHNIQUES: STRETCHING, FOAM ROLLING, ETC.

Active recovery techniques are valuable tools for facilitating muscle recovery and preventing stiffness. These methods promote blood flow, reduce muscle soreness, and aid in overall recovery.

1. **Stretching:**
   - *Static Stretching*: This involves holding a stretch for 15-60 seconds to improve flexibility and reduce muscle tension. Static stretching should be incorporated into your post-workout routine to enhance muscle relaxation and prevent stiffness. Common stretches include hamstring stretches, quadriceps stretches, and shoulder stretches.
   - *Dynamic Stretching*: Performed before workouts, dynamic stretching helps prepare muscles and joints for exercise. It involves controlled movements that increase range of motion and reduce the risk of injury. Examples include leg swings, arm circles, and hip rotations.
2. **Foam Rolling:**
   - *Self-Myofascial Release*: Foam rolling is a technique used for self-myofascial release, which helps release muscle knots and improve blood flow. By applying pressure to areas of tightness or discomfort, foam rolling can aid in recovery and reduce soreness. It

is particularly effective for areas like the lower back, thighs, and calves.
- *Techniques*: To foam roll effectively, apply moderate pressure and move slowly over each muscle group for 1-2 minutes. Focus on areas of high tension, but avoid excessive pressure to prevent discomfort. Incorporating foam rolling into your routine can enhance recovery and flexibility.

3. **Other Techniques:**
   - *Yoga*: Yoga integrates stretching, breathing, and relaxation techniques that promote flexibility, balance, and mental relaxation. Regular yoga practice can support overall recovery by reducing muscle stiffness and enhancing flexibility. Consider incorporating yoga sessions into your weekly routine to complement your weight-lifting program.
   - *Light Cardio*: Engaging in low-intensity activities such as walking or cycling can enhance circulation and aid in the removal of metabolic waste products from muscles. Light cardio sessions, lasting 20-30 minutes, can be beneficial for recovery and overall fitness.

MANAGING FATIGUE AND OVERTRAINING

Managing fatigue and preventing overtraining are essential for maintaining progress and preventing injury. Overtraining occurs when the body is subjected to excessive training without adequate recovery, leading to diminished performance and increased injury risk.

1. **Signs of Overtraining:**
   - *Physical Symptoms:* Common signs of overtraining include persistent muscle soreness, decreased performance, increased susceptibility to illness, and disrupted sleep patterns. These symptoms indicate that the body may not be fully recovering between workouts.
   - *Mental Symptoms*: Overtraining can also manifest as mental symptoms such as irritability, lack of motivation, and difficulty concentrating. These psychological effects can negatively impact training consistency and performance.
2. **Strategies to Prevent Overtraining:**
   - *Balanced Program*: Ensure that your training program includes a balance of intensity, volume, and recovery time. Incorporate rest days and vary workouts to prevent excessive strain on the body. A well-structured program helps avoid overtraining and supports long-term progress.
   - *Listen to Your Body*: Pay close attention to signs of fatigue and adjust your training accordingly. If you experience persistent soreness, decreased performance, or lack of motivation, consider scaling back your workouts or adding more rest days to promote recovery.
3. **Recovery Techniques:**

Scheduled Rest Days: Include regular rest days in your training program to allow your body to recover and adapt. Rest days are crucial for muscle repair and overall recovery, and they should be planned into your weekly routine.

Deload Weeks: Implement periodic deload weeks, where you reduce the intensity and volume of your workouts. Deload weeks help prevent overtraining and provide an opportunity for recovery. They can be scheduled every 4-6 weeks or based on individual needs.

THE ROLE OF MASSAGE AND PHYSIOTHERAPY

Massage and physiotherapy can play a significant role in enhancing recovery, reducing muscle soreness, and addressing any injuries or imbalances. These interventions provide targeted relief and support overall well-being.

1. **Massage:**
   - *Benefits*: Massage therapy increases blood flow, reduces muscle tension, and promotes relaxation. It can aid in recovery by alleviating soreness and improving overall flexibility. Regular massage sessions can be beneficial for maintaining muscle health and preventing stiffness.
   - *Types*: Different types of massage, such as Swedish, deep tissue, and sports massage, offer various benefits. Sports massage, in particular, targets muscle groups used during weight-lifting and can help reduce post-workout soreness and improve recovery.
2. **Physiotherapy:**
   - *Assessment and Treatment*: Physiotherapists assess and address movement imbalances, muscle imbalances, and injuries. They provide personalized treatment plans that may include exercises, manual

therapy techniques, and lifestyle recommendations to aid in recovery and prevent future issues.
- *Rehabilitation*: For individuals recovering from injuries, physiotherapy is essential for regaining strength, flexibility, and function. Physiotherapists develop tailored rehabilitation programs to ensure proper healing and a safe return to training.

3. **Integrating Massage and Physiotherapy:**
   - *Routine*: Incorporate regular massage sessions into your recovery routine, especially during periods of intense training or after significant lifting sessions. This can help maintain muscle health and support overall recovery.
   - *Consultation*: If you experience persistent pain, discomfort, or movement issues, consult with a qualified physiotherapist. They can provide targeted interventions and strategies for effective recovery and injury prevention.

Incorporating effective recovery strategies into your weight-lifting regimen is crucial for optimizing performance and achieving long-term success. By prioritizing sleep, utilizing active recovery techniques, managing fatigue, and seeking professional assistance when needed, you can enhance muscle recovery, prevent injury, and ensure continued progress in your training journey. Proper recovery not only supports muscle growth and strength but also contributes to overall health and well-being, ensuring that you can perform at your best and achieve your fitness goals.

SECTION FIVE

THE MENTAL GAME AND COMPETITION

14

THE PSYCHOLOGY OF WEIGHT-LIFTING

WEIGHT-LIFTING IS NOT MERELY A TEST OF physical strength; it is equally a challenge of mental fortitude and psychological resilience. The mental aspects of weight-lifting can profoundly impact performance, recovery, and overall success. This chapter explores the critical psychological strategies for excelling in weight-lifting, including building mental toughness and focus, the role of visualization and goal setting, dealing with plateaus and setbacks, and developing a winning mindset.

BUILDING MENTAL TOUGHNESS AND FOCUS

Mental toughness and focus are foundational for overcoming challenges and achieving success in weight-lifting. They enable you to push through physical and psychological barriers, maintain motivation, and perform optimally under pressure.

1. **Defining Mental Toughness:**
   - *Resilience*: Mental toughness is characterized by resilience—the ability to recover quickly from setbacks and maintain performance despite adversity. Resilient lifters can bounce back from disappointments, stay committed during tough training phases, and persist through plateaus.
   - *Commitment*: A mentally tough individual remains steadfastly committed to their training goals. This commitment involves not only showing up for workouts but also adhering to a disciplined regimen, managing nutrition and recovery, and consistently striving for improvement.
2. **Strategies to Build Mental Toughness:**
   - *Positive Self-Talk*: Engage in positive self-talk to enhance confidence and maintain a constructive mindset. Replace self-doubt and negative thoughts with affirmations that reinforce your strengths and capabilities. For instance, rather than thinking "I'm not strong enough," tell yourself "I am improving every day and capable of reaching my goals."
   - *Embracing Challenges*: Regularly set and tackle new challenges to build mental resilience. Challenging yourself with progressively harder workouts and heavier weights helps you become accustomed to pushing your limits and embracing discomfort as part of growth.
   - *Mindfulness and Focus*: Practice mindfulness techniques, such as meditation and deep breathing, to improve concentration and presence during training. Mindfulness helps you stay focused on

the task at hand, reducing stress and enhancing performance. Techniques like visualizing your lifts and controlling your breathing can significantly improve focus and execution.

THE ROLE OF VISUALIZATION AND GOAL SETTING

Visualization and goal setting are potent psychological tools that can significantly impact your weight-lifting journey. They help you mentally prepare for challenges, stay motivated, and achieve your objectives.

1. **Visualization:**
     - *Mental Rehearsal*: Visualization involves mentally rehearsing your lifts and workouts. By vividly imagining yourself executing a lift with perfect form and technique, you create a mental blueprint that can improve actual performance. Visualization helps reinforce correct technique and boosts confidence by familiarizing you with the desired outcome.
     - *Positive Imagery*: Use positive imagery to foster confidence and motivation. Visualize not only the physical act of lifting but also the emotions and sensations associated with achieving your goals. Imagine the satisfaction and pride of hitting a new personal best or successfully completing a challenging workout.
2. **Goal Setting:**
     - *SMART Goals:* Set Specific, Measurable, Achievable, Relevant, and Time-bound (SMART) goals to guide

your training. SMART goals provide clarity and direction, making it easier to track progress and stay motivated. For example, instead of setting a vague goal like "get stronger," aim for "increase my squat by 20 pounds in the next three months."
- *Short-Term and Long-Term Goals*: Establish both short-term and long-term goals. Short-term goals offer immediate milestones and quick wins, while long-term goals provide a broader vision of your overall progress. Break long-term goals into smaller, actionable steps to maintain focus and motivation throughout your training.

DEALING WITH PLATEAUS AND SETBACKS

Plateaus and setbacks are inevitable in weight-lifting, but how you respond to them can determine your continued success. Developing strategies to manage these challenges is crucial for sustained progress and motivation.

1. **Understanding Plateaus:**
   - *Causes*: Plateaus occur when progress stalls despite consistent effort. Common causes include inadequate recovery, lack of variety in training, or reaching genetic limits. Recognizing the underlying cause of a plateau helps in implementing effective strategies to overcome it.
   - *Strategies for Overcoming Plateaus*: Incorporate variations in your training routine to break through plateaus. This may involve changing exercise variations, adjusting training intensity, or

experimenting with different rep and set schemes. For example, if your squat progress has stalled, consider incorporating front squats or adding pause squats to your routine.

2. **Handling Setbacks:**
   - *Acceptance and Adaptation*: Accept setbacks as a natural part of the training process. Instead of viewing setbacks as failures, see them as opportunities for growth and learning. Analyze what went wrong and adapt your approach accordingly, whether that means revising your training program, adjusting your goals, or addressing any technical issues.
   - *Maintaining Motivation*: Stay motivated by focusing on your achievements and progress rather than dwelling on setbacks. Remind yourself of your long-term goals and the reasons why you started lifting in the first place. Engaging in positive self-talk, celebrating small victories, and seeking support from training partners can help maintain motivation during challenging times.

DEVELOPING A WINNING MINDSET

A winning mindset is a powerful psychological attribute that drives success and helps you overcome obstacles. Cultivating this mindset involves developing qualities such as determination, perseverance, and self-belief.

1. **Cultivating Determination:**
   - *Drive and Persistence*: Develop a strong sense of determination and persistence. Stay committed to

your training program even when progress is slow or obstacles arise. Embrace challenges as opportunities to improve and grow stronger. A determined mindset helps you push through difficulties and stay focused on your long-term goals.
- *Passion and Enthusiasm*: Cultivate a genuine passion for weight-lifting. Approach each workout with enthusiasm and a positive attitude. Your excitement and dedication will not only enhance your performance but also make the training process more enjoyable.

2. **Fostering Self-Belief:**
    - *Confidence Building*: Build self-confidence by setting and achieving realistic goals, celebrating your successes, and focusing on your strengths. Confidence comes from recognizing your accomplishments and acknowledging your progress. Engage in activities that reinforce your self-belief, such as tracking your improvements and reflecting on past successes.
    - *Embracing a Growth Mindset*: Adopt a growth mindset, which emphasizes learning and development over fixed abilities. View challenges and setbacks as opportunities to learn and improve rather than as reflections of your limitations. A growth mindset encourages you to persist in the face of difficulties and continuously strive for improvement.

In conclusion, understanding and leveraging the psychological aspects of weight-lifting can greatly enhance your training experience and performance. By building mental toughness, utilizing visualization and goal setting, addressing plateaus and setbacks effectively, and developing a winning mindset, you can overcome obstacles, stay motivated, and achieve your weight-lifting goals. The power of the mind is a critical component of success in weight-lifting, and harnessing its potential is key to reaching new heights in your fitness journey. Embrace the psychological challenges and opportunities that weight-lifting presents, and use them to fuel your progress and personal growth.

15

PREPARING FOR COMPETITIONS

PREPARING FOR WEIGHT-LIFTING COMPETITIONS involves more than just physical training. It requires a comprehensive approach that includes understanding different types of competitions, training effectively, utilizing support from coaches and training partners, and knowing what to expect on the competition day. This chapter provides detailed insights into each of these areas, helping you navigate the path from preparation to performance.

UNDERSTANDING THE DIFFERENT TYPES OF COMPETITIONS

Weight-lifting competitions vary widely, each with its unique format, rules, and demands. Familiarizing yourself with these differences is crucial for effective preparation and performance.

1. **Powerlifting Competitions:**
    - *Overview*: Powerlifting competitions focus on three main lifts: the squat, bench press, and deadlift.

Competitors are judged based on the maximum weight they can lift in each of these exercises.
- *Format*: Athletes perform each lift in a specific order, with three attempts per lift. The highest successful lift in each category is recorded, and the lifter with the highest total weight across all three lifts wins.
- *Preparation*: Training for powerlifting involves developing strength and technique in the three core lifts. Emphasis is placed on maximizing strength and perfecting form to achieve the highest possible lifts on competition day.

2. **Olympic Weightlifting Competitions:**
   - *Overview*: Olympic weightlifting competitions feature two main lifts: the snatch and the clean and jerk. These lifts require a combination of strength, power, technique, and speed.
   - *Format*: Athletes have three attempts at each lift, with the highest successful attempt recorded. The lifter with the highest total combined weight from both lifts wins.
   - *Preparation*: Training for Olympic weightlifting focuses on developing explosive power, technique, and flexibility. Training often includes a combination of strength work, technique drills, and Olympic lift variations.

3. **Bodybuilding Competitions:**
   - *Overview*: Bodybuilding competitions emphasize muscle development, symmetry, and aesthetics. Competitors are judged on their physique through a series of poses and routines.
   - *Format*: Athletes perform a mandatory posing

routine, showcasing their muscle definition and symmetry. The judging is based on overall muscle size, proportion, and presentation.
- *Preparation*: Preparation for bodybuilding involves a combination of resistance training, hypertrophy-focused workouts, strict dieting, and posing practice. The goal is to build muscle mass while reducing body fat to achieve a well-defined physique.

4. **CrossFit Competitions:**
   - *Overview*: CrossFit competitions test a wide range of fitness elements, including strength, endurance, and skill through varied workouts known as WODs (Workouts of the Day).
   - *Format*: Competitors complete a series of workouts, which may include weight-lifting, cardiovascular exercises, and bodyweight movements. Scoring is based on performance in these varied workouts.
   - *Preparation*: Training for CrossFit competitions involves a diverse approach, focusing on overall fitness, strength, conditioning, and skill development across multiple domains.

WHAT TO EXPECT ON COMPETITION DAY

Understanding what to expect on competition day helps you prepare mentally and physically for the event. Here's a breakdown of common elements and how to navigate them effectively:

1. **Arrival and Check-In:**
   - *Arrival Time*: Arrive early to familiarize yourself with the venue and complete check-in procedures.

This allows you to get settled and reduce any pre-competition anxiety.
- *Weigh-In*: For weight-class-based competitions, participate in the weigh-in process. Ensure that you meet the weight requirements for your class and manage any last-minute adjustments to your weight.

2. **Warm-Up and Preparation:**
   - *Warm-Up Routine*: Follow a structured warm-up routine to prepare your body for lifting. This includes dynamic stretching, mobility exercises, and progressively heavier warm-up sets.
   - *Mental Preparation*: Use visualization and positive self-talk to mentally prepare for your lifts. Focus on your technique, strategy, and performance goals to stay confident and composed.

3. **During the Competition:**
   - *Attempt Selection*: Work with your coach to select your attempts based on your current strength levels and competition strategy. Make strategic choices that maximize your performance and increase your chances of success.
   - *Adherence to Rules*: Adhere to the competition rules and guidelines, including proper lifting techniques, attire, and equipment. Familiarize yourself with the judging criteria and ensure that you comply with all requirements.

4. **Post-Competition:**
   - *Reflect and Review:* After the competition, take time to reflect on your performance and review feedback from judges and coaches. Identify areas for improvement and celebrate your achievements.

- *Recovery and Rest*: Prioritize recovery and rest following the competition. Allow your body and mind to recover from the physical and emotional demands of the event.

By following a structured preparation plan and approaching the competition with confidence and clarity, you can enhance your performance and achieve your goals.

16

ANALYZING PERFORMANCE AND IMPROVEMENT

TO EXCEL IN WEIGHT-LIFTING, CONTINUOUS ANALYSIS and refinement of performance are crucial. This chapter focuses on methods for reviewing and analyzing your lifts, using video analysis for technical improvements, adjusting training based on performance data, and learning from failures and injuries. By applying these strategies, you can enhance your lifting technique, optimize your training regimen, and achieve sustained progress in your weight-lifting journey.

REVIEWING LIFTS AND ANALYZING TECHNIQUE

Effective analysis of your lifts is key to identifying areas for improvement and ensuring that your technique is optimized for performance and safety.

1. **Self-Assessment:**
   - *Immediate Feedback*: After each lift, take a moment

to reflect on how it felt. Consider aspects such as technique, effort, and any discomfort or difficulty experienced. This immediate feedback can offer insights into areas that need adjustment.
- *Journaling*: Maintain a lifting journal where you record details of each session, including weights lifted, sets, reps, and any observations about your technique or performance. This log helps track progress and identify patterns or recurring issues.

2. **Technique Analysis:**
   - *Key Components*: Break down your lifts into key components, such as setup, execution, and finishing. Analyze each component to ensure proper form and technique. For example, in the squat, assess your foot placement, depth, knee alignment, and overall movement pattern.
   - *Coaching Input*: Seek feedback from experienced coaches or training partners who can provide an external perspective on your technique. They can offer valuable insights and corrective cues to refine your lifting form.

USING VIDEO ANALYSIS FOR IMPROVEMENT

Video analysis is a powerful tool for detailed examination of your lifting technique and performance. It provides visual feedback that can enhance your understanding and facilitate improvements.

1. **Recording Your Lifts:**
   - *Equipment*: Use a high-quality camera or smartphone to record your lifts from multiple angles. This allows

you to capture different perspectives and assess your technique more thoroughly.
- *Angles to Consider*: Record lifts from side, front, and back views to analyze different aspects of your technique. For instance, a side view can help you evaluate your bar path and body alignment, while a front view can show knee tracking and foot placement.

2. **Analyzing the Footage:**
   - *Slow Motion*: Use slow-motion playback to examine your lifting technique in detail. Slow-motion helps identify subtle errors in form that may not be visible in real-time.
   - *Comparative Analysis*: Compare your footage to that of experienced lifters or instructional videos. Look for differences in technique and adjust your form accordingly. Pay attention to aspects such as bar path, body positioning, and movement efficiency.

3. **Setting Goals Based on Analysis:**
   - *Identify Weaknesses*: Use video analysis to pinpoint specific areas of weakness or technical flaws. For example, if you notice that your back is rounding during the deadlift, focus on improving your spinal alignment and core stability.
   - *Create Action Plans*: Develop action plans to address identified issues. Set specific, measurable goals for improvement and incorporate drills or exercises into your training to target these areas.

ADJUSTING TRAINING BASED ON PERFORMANCE DATA

Regularly reviewing performance data allows you to make informed adjustments to your training regimen, ensuring that your program remains effective and aligned with your goals.

1. **Tracking Performance Metrics:**
    - *Recording Data*: Keep detailed records of your performance metrics, including weights lifted, volume, intensity, and progression over time. Track both strength gains and technical improvements.
    - *Analyzing Trends*: Analyze trends in your performance data to identify patterns and make data-driven decisions. For example, if you notice consistent difficulty with certain weights or exercises, it may indicate a need for targeted intervention.
2. **Adjusting Training Variables:**
    - *Intensity and Volume*: Modify training intensity and volume based on your performance data. For example, if you are consistently hitting new personal bests, you may need to increase the intensity or adjust the volume to continue progressing.
    - *Exercise Selection*: Adjust your exercise selection based on performance analysis. If certain lifts or variations are showing significant progress, consider incorporating more of those into your routine.
3. **Periodization and Progression:**
    - *Implementing Periodization*: Use periodization techniques to structure your training program in

phases that focus on different aspects, such as strength, hypertrophy, and power. Adjust these phases based on your performance data and goals.
- *Progression Planning*: Plan for progression by setting incremental goals and adjusting your training loads accordingly. Ensure that your program includes progressive overload to continuously challenge your muscles and stimulate growth.

Embrace the process of self-assessment and growth as a crucial component of your weight-lifting journey, and use these insights to drive ongoing progress and excellence.

17

NURTURING A FUTURE OLYMPIC WEIGHTLIFTER

OLYMPIC WEIGHTLIFTING IS A SPORT THAT DEMANDS strength, technique, mental focus, and years of disciplined training. Nurturing a young athlete into a future Olympic weightlifter requires proper guidance, early engagement in strength training, and building both physical and mental resilience.

EARLY EXPOSURE TO STRENGTH TRAINING

Start with General Fitness: Before diving into specific weightlifting movements, introduce kids to general fitness and bodyweight exercises like squats, push-ups, and pull-ups. This helps them build a solid foundation of strength, balance, and coordination, which are essential in weightlifting.

Age-Appropriate Training: While younger children shouldn't engage in heavy weightlifting, they can begin learning the basic movements—like squats, deadlifts, and presses—with light weights or PVC pipes. Emphasize technique over weight to avoid injury and ensure they build the right habits early.

FINDING THE RIGHT COACH AND GYM

Qualified Coaching: A specialized weightlifting coach is crucial for developing proper form and technique. Look for someone with experience in Olympic lifting who understands how to safely progress young athletes in their training.

Weightlifting-Friendly Environment: It's essential to train in a gym that supports Olympic weightlifting and has the proper equipment, such as barbells, bumper plates, platforms, and squat racks. The right environment promotes safety, technique, and a supportive lifting community.

PHYSICAL CONDITIONING FOR WEIGHTLIFTING

Strength Building: As they grow older and become more proficient in technique, introduce weight gradually to build their strength. Core exercises like squats, deadlifts, and overhead presses are essential to overall strength development and should be a regular part of their training.

Mobility and Flexibility: Flexibility and mobility are crucial for successful weightlifting, as lifts like the snatch and clean require a full range of motion. Incorporate stretching routines, mobility drills, and yoga to maintain and enhance flexibility.

Power and Speed: Olympic weightlifting is about explosive power. Drills that focus on developing speed and explosiveness, such as jumping exercises, sprinting, or medicine ball throws, are valuable additions to training.

MENTAL TOUGHNESS AND FOCUS

Building Mental Resilience: Olympic weightlifting can be physically taxing and mentally challenging. Young athletes must learn to stay focused under pressure and develop mental toughness, especially during intense training cycles and competitions.

Goal Setting and Progress Tracking: Encourage weightlifters to set realistic short-term and long-term goals. Whether it's improving a specific lift or reaching a certain weight class, having goals helps them stay motivated and focused.

Visualization and Mental Rehearsal: Teach them the importance of visualization techniques, where they mentally rehearse their lifts and performances. This helps build confidence and reduce anxiety during competitions.

NUTRITION AND RECOVERY

Proper Fueling: Olympic weightlifters need to consume a diet rich in protein, complex carbohydrates, and healthy fats to fuel their training and muscle recovery. Ensuring they get enough calories is crucial, especially for young athletes who are growing and training hard.

Recovery and Rest: Rest is just as important as training. Ensure that young athletes get enough sleep (8–10 hours per night) and include rest days in their training schedule. Recovery techniques like foam rolling, massage, and stretching will help reduce soreness and prevent injuries.

THE PATH TO THE OLYMPICS

Commitment to the Process: Olympic weightlifting is a long-term commitment. Ensure the young athlete understands that progression takes time and consistent effort. Celebrate incremental improvements, but also encourage them to remain patient.

Competitions and Exposure: Start by entering local and regional competitions. As they advance, aim for national-level meets to gain recognition and experience. Higher competition levels are essential for building confidence and understanding the rigors of elite-level competition.

Staying Focused: The road to the Olympics is long and challenging. Maintaining a balance of passion, discipline, and resilience is crucial to making it to the elite level in weightlifting.

18

FILIPINO OLYMPIANS IN WEIGHTLIFTING: LIFTING THE NATION

WEIGHTLIFTING HAS LONG BEEN A SOURCE OF pride for the Philippines, with its athletes showing extraordinary strength and determination on the Olympic stage. Filipino weightlifters have not only qualified for multiple Olympic Games but have also brought home medals, elevating the sport's profile in the country. This chapter explores the journey of Filipino Olympians in weightlifting, highlighting the trailblazers and their inspiring stories of grit and triumph.

EARLY PIONEERS

The Philippines first made a mark in Olympic weightlifting in the mid-20th century. **Rodrigo del Rosario** was the first Filipino weightlifter to compete in the Olympics, representing the country in the 1948 London Games. Though he did not medal, Del Rosario's participation was a historic moment that sparked interest in weightlifting across the nation.

In the years that followed, Filipino weightlifters began to make their presence known on the international stage. **Salvador del Rosario**, who competed in the 1964 Tokyo Olympics, was another pioneer who helped shape the future of the sport in the Philippines. Although he faced fierce competition, his efforts helped pave the way for future generations, proving that Filipino athletes had the potential to succeed in the power and precision sport of weightlifting.

THE RISE OF FEMALE WEIGHTLIFTERS

The turning point for Filipino weightlifting came in the 21st century, with the rise of female weightlifters who brought the sport to new heights. One name stands out above the rest: **Hidilyn Diaz**. Diaz's journey from humble beginnings to Olympic glory is a story of relentless perseverance and unshakable determination.

Hidilyn Diaz

Hidilyn first competed in the 2008 Beijing Olympics at the age of 17, where she became the first female weightlifter to represent the Philippines. Although she did not medal in her Olympic debut, she gained invaluable experience that would fuel her desire to reach the podium. In the 2012 London Olympics, Diaz competed again, finishing in the top ten of her weight class but still falling short of a medal.

Undeterred by her setbacks, Hidilyn Diaz trained even harder and made history at the 2016 Rio de Janeiro Olympics by winning a silver medal in the women's 53kg category. This victory marked the first time in 20 years that the Philippines had won an Olympic medal and the first ever in weightlifting. Diaz's silver medal was a monumental achievement for Filipino sports, and it reignited the nation's passion for the sport of weightlifting.

But Diaz wasn't done yet. At the **2020 Tokyo Olympics**, she achieved the ultimate triumph by winning the country's first-ever Olympic gold medal. Competing in the women's 55kg weight class, Diaz lifted a total of 224 kg, setting an Olympic record in the clean and jerk. Her victory was celebrated across the Philippines, cementing her status as one of the greatest Filipino athletes of all time. Diaz's gold medal not only brought pride to the country but also inspired a new generation of Filipino athletes to pursue their dreams.

Hidilyn Diaz, Stamp of 2021 Tokyo Olympic Medalists

EMERGING TALENTS IN WEIGHTLIFTING

Hidilyn Diaz's success has sparked a surge of interest in weightlifting in the Philippines, with many young athletes now aspiring to follow in her footsteps. **Elreen Ando**, who competed alongside Diaz in the 2020 Tokyo Olympics, is one of the most promising rising stars in the sport. Competing in the women's 64kg category, Ando placed seventh in her Olympic debut, a remarkable feat for a young athlete on her first trip to the world's biggest sporting stage. Her impressive performance shows that Filipino weightlifting has a bright future ahead.

In the men's division, Filipino lifters have also been

Elreen Ando at the 2020 Summer Olympics

making strides. **Nestor Colonia**, who competed in the men's 56kg category at the 2016 Rio Olympics, was one of the top weightlifters in Southeast Asia. Although he didn't bring home a medal, his performance was a reminder that the Philippines has talented male weightlifters capable of competing on the global stage.

Nestor Colonia

The Philippine Weightlifting Association (PWA) has also been instrumental in supporting the development of the sport, providing training opportunities and international exposure for athletes. Thanks to the efforts of organizations like the PWA and individual coaches and supporters, Filipino weightlifters are now better equipped to compete on the world stage.

THE FUTURE OF FILIPINO WEIGHTLIFTING

With the success of Hidilyn Diaz and the emergence of new talents like Elreen Ando, the future of Filipino weightlifting looks brighter than ever. As more young athletes take up the sport, inspired by the achievements of their Olympian predecessors, the Philippines has the potential to become a powerhouse in weightlifting on the global stage.

CONCLUSION

The future of weightlifting is set for an exciting transformation driven by advancements in technique, technology, and global engagement. Personalized training programs will enhance efficiency while wearable devices and biomechanical analysis provide valuable feedback. The sport's global growth, fueled by international competitions and online resources, fosters cross-cultural influences and innovative practices. Looking ahead, hybrid-training approaches will gain traction, alongside a focus on overall health and wellness. Efforts to promote inclusivity and sustainability will further enrich the community. By embracing these changes, lifters can continue to push performance boundaries and contribute to a vibrant future in weightlifting.

LIST OF OLYMPIC MEDALISTS (2000–2024)

MEN

Featherweight

Games	Gold	Silver	Bronze
2000 Sydney	Nikolaj Pešalov Croatia	Leonidas Sabanis Greece	Gennady Oleshchuk Belarus
2004 Athens	Shi Zhiyong China	Le Maosheng China	Israel José Rubio Venezuela
2008 Beijing	Zhang Xiangxiang China	Diego Salazar Colombia	Triyatno Indonesia
2012 London	Kim Un-guk North Korea	Óscar Figueroa Colombia	Eko Yuli Irawan Indonesia
2016 Rio de Janeiro	Óscar Figueroa Colombia	Eko Yuli Irawan Indonesia	Farkhad Kharki Kazakhstan
2020 Tokyo	Chen Lijun China	Luis Javier Mosquera Colombia	Mirko Zanni Italy
2024 Paris	Li Fabin China	Theerapong Silachai Thailand	Hampton Morris United States

LIST OF OLYMPIC MEDALISTS (2000–2024)

Lightweight

Games	Gold	Silver	Bronze
2000 Sydney	Galabin Boevski Bulgaria	Georgi Markov Bulgaria	Siarhei Laurenau Belarus
2004 Athens	Zhang Guozheng China	Lee Bae-young South Korea	Nikolaj Pešalov Croatia
2008 Beijing	Liao Hui China	Vencelas Dabaya France	Yordanis Borrero Cuba
2012 London	Lin Qingfeng China	Triyatno Indonesia	Kim Myong-hyok North Korea
2016 Rio de Janeiro	Shi Zhiyong China	Daniyar Ismayilov Turkey	Luis Javier Mosquera Colombia
2020 Tokyo	Shi Zhiyong China	Julio Mayora Venezuela	Rahmat Erwin Abdullah Indonesia
2024 Paris	Rizki Juniansyah Indonesia	Weeraphon Wichuma Thailand	Bozhidar Andreev Bulgaria

Middleweight

Games	Gold	Silver	Bronze
2000 Sydney	Zhan Xugang China	Viktor Mitrou Greece	Arsen Melikyan Armenia
2004 Athens	Taner Sağır Turkey	Sergey Filimonov Kazakhstan	Reyhan Arabacıoğlu Turkey
2008 Beijing	Sa Jae-hyouk South Korea	Li Hongli China	Gevorg Davtyan Armenia

LIST OF OLYMPIC MEDALISTS (2000-2024)

Games	Gold	Silver	Bronze
2012 London	Lü Xiaojun China	Lu Haojie China	Iván Cambar Cuba
2016 Rio de Janeiro	Lü Xiaojun China	Mohamed Ihab Egypt	Chatuphum Chinnawong Thailand
2020 Tokyo	Lü Xiaojun China	Zacarías Bonnat Dominican Republic	Antonino Pizzolato Italy
2024 Paris	Karlos Nasar Bulgaria	Yeison López Colombia	Antonino Pizzolato Italy

Heavyweight

Games	Gold	Silver	Bronze
2000 Sydney	Hossein Tavakkoli Iran	Alan Tsagaev Bulgaria	Said Saif Asaad Qatar
2004 Athens	Dmitry Berestov Russia	Ihor Razoronov Ukraine	Gleb Pisarevskiy Russia
2008 Beijing	Andrei Aramnau Belarus	Dmitry Klokov Russia	Marcin Dołęga Poland
2012 London	Navab Nassirshalal Iran	Bartłomiej Bonk Poland	Ivan Efremov Uzbekistan
2016 Rio de Janeiro	Ruslan Nurudinov Uzbekistan	Simon Martirosyan Armenia	Aleksandr Zaychikov Kazakhstan
2020 Tokyo	Akbar Djuraev Uzbekistan	Simon Martirosyan Armenia	Artūrs Plēsnieks Latvia
2024 Paris	Liu Huanhua China	Akbar Djuraev Uzbekistan	Yauheni Tsikhantsou Individual Neutral Athletes

LIST OF OLYMPIC MEDALISTS (2000–2024)

Super heavyweight

Games	Gold	Silver	Bronze
2000 Sydney	Hossein Rezazadeh Iran	Ronny Weller Germany	Andrei Chemerkin Russia
2004 Athens	Hossein Rezazadeh Iran	Viktors Ščerbatihs Latvia	Velichko Cholakov Bulgaria
2008 Beijing	Matthias Steiner Germany	Evgeny Chigishev Russia	Viktors Ščerbatihs Latvia
2012 London	Behdad Salimi Iran	Sajjad Anoushiravani Iran	Jeon Sang-guen South Korea
2016 Rio de Janeiro	Lasha Talakhadze Georgia	Gor Minasyan Armenia	Irakli Turmanidze Georgia
2020 Tokyo	Lasha Talakhadze Georgia	Ali Davoudi Iran	Man Asaad Syria
2024 Paris	Lasha Talakhadze Georgia	Varazdat Lalayan Armenia	Gor Minasyan Bahrain

WOMEN

Flyweight

Games	Gold	Silver	Bronze
2000 Sydney	Tara Nott United States	Raema Lisa Rumbewas Indonesia	Sri Indriyani Indonesia
2004 Athens	Nurcan Taylan Turkey	Li Zhuo China	Aree Wiratthaworn Thailand
2008 Beijing	Chen Wei-ling Chinese Taipei	Im Jyoung-hwa South Korea	Pensiri Laosirikul Thailand

Games	Gold	Silver	Bronze
2012 London	Wang Mingjuan China	Hiromi Miyake Japan	Ryang Chun-hwa North Korea
2016 Rio de Janeiro	Sopita Tanasan Thailand	Sri Wahyuni Agustiani Indonesia	Hiromi Miyake Japan
2020 Tokyo	Hou Zhihui China	Saikhom Mirabai Chanu India	Windy Cantika Aisah Indonesia
2024 Paris	Hou Zhihui China	Mihaela Cambei Romania	Surodchana Khambao Thailand

Lightweight

Games	Gold	Silver	Bronze
2000 Sydney	Soraya Jiménez Mexico	Ri Song Hui North Korea	Khassaraporn Suta Thailand
2004 Athens	Chen Yanqing China	Ri Song Hui North Korea	Wandee Kameaim Thailand
2008 Beijing	Chen Yanqing China	O Jong Ae North Korea	Wandee Kameaim Thailand
2012 London	Li Xueying China	Pimsiri Sirikaew Thailand	Rattikan Gulnoi Thailand
2016 Rio de Janeiro details	Sukanya Srisurat Thailand	Pimsiri Sirikaew Thailand	Kuo Hsing-chun Chinese Taipei
2020 Tokyo	Kuo Hsing-chun Chinese Taipei	Polina Guryeva Turkmenistan	Mikiko Ando Japan
2024 Paris	Luo Shifang China	Maude Charron Canada	Kuo Hsing-chun Chinese Taipei

LIST OF OLYMPIC MEDALISTS (2000–2024)

Light Heavyweight

Games	Gold	Silver	Bronze
2000 Sydney	Lin Weining China	Erzsébet Márkus Hungary	Karnam Malleswari India
2004 Athens	Liu Chunhong China	Eszter Krutzler Hungary	Zarema Kasaeva Russia
2008 Beijing	Oksana Slivenko Russia	Leydi Solís Colombia	Abeer Abdelrahman Egypt
2012 London	Rim Jong-sim North Korea	Anna Nurmukhambetova Kazakhstan	Ubaldina Valoyes Colombia
2016 Rio de Janeiro	Xiang Yanmei China	Zhazira Zhapparkul Kazakhstan	Sara Ahmed Egypt
2020 Tokyo	Neisi Dajomes Ecuador	Katherine Nye United States	Aremi Fuentes Mexico
2024 Paris	Olivia Reeves United States	Mari Sánchez Colombia	Angie Palacios Ecuador

Heavyweight

Games	Gold	Silver	Bronze
2000 Sydney	María Isabel Urrutia Colombia	Ruth Ogbeifo Nigeria	Kuo Yi-hang Chinese Taipei
2004 Athens	Pawina Thongsuk Thailand	Natalya Zabolotnaya Russia	Valentina Popova Russia
2008 Beijing	Alla Vazhenina Kazakhstan	Lydia Valentín Spain	Damaris Aguirre Mexico
2012 London	Lydia Valentín Spain	Abeer Abdelrahman Egypt	Madias Nzesso Cameroon

Games	Gold	Silver	Bronze
2016 Rio de Janeiro	Rim Jong-sim North Korea	Darya Naumava Belarus	Lydia Valentín Spain
2020 Tokyo	Wang Zhouyu China	Tamara Salazar Ecuador	Crismery Santana Dominican Republic
2024 Paris	Solfrid Koanda Norway	Sara Ahmed Egypt	Neisi Dajomes Ecuador

Super Heavyweight

Games	Gold	Silver	Bronze
2000 Sydney	Ding Meiyuan China	Agata Wróbel Poland	Cheryl Haworth United States
2004 Athens	Tang Gonghong China	Jang Mi-ran South Korea	Agata Wróbel Poland
2008 Beijing	Jang Mi-ran South Korea	Ele Opeloge Samoa	Mariam Usman Nigeria
2012 London	Zhou Lulu China	Tatiana Kashirina Russia	Jang Mi-ran South Korea
2016 Rio de Janeiro	Meng Suping China	Kim Kuk-hyang North Korea	Sarah Robles United States
2020 Tokyo	Li Wenwen China	Emily Campbell Great Britain	Sarah Robles United States
2024 Paris	Li Wenwen China	Park Hye-jeong South Korea	Emily Campbell Great Britain